THE EXPERIENCE OF YOUNG ADULTS

THE EXPERIENCE OF YOUNG ADULTS

EDITED BY STEPHEN J. GOLBURGH

SCHENKMAN PUBLISHING COMPANY, INC.

CAMBRIDGE

Schenkman books are distributed by
General Learning Press
250 James Street
Morristown, New Jersey

DEDICATION

To the Memory of my Father,
M. Harry Golburgh

CONTENTS

PREFACE

Life is the process of keeping constructively, joyfully, and creatively occupied in order to live as fully as possible and thus change and grow.

Stephen J. Golburgh

Many textbooks dealing with youth explain only segments of the youth's behavior. In reading them, one rarely gets a picture of a real person. One learns something about people's intellectual changes over a period of years, or something about their physiology, or how they might be more scientifically studied. But the person is hardly visible. He is buried beneath charts, statistics, and intellectual and general conceptions.

One function of the psychology instructor is to help his students to understand a person, or, more specifically in this case, the young person as a living, feeling, real, human individual. Yet we seem to get very few books that attempt to do this. One might ask why this is so. Perhaps some psychologists, being human, are fearful of whole people and their experiences and anxieties as they see and express them. Perhaps they are fearful because material of this sort arouses in them anxiety which makes them uncomfortable. Often they feel that this type of material is more than their students can tolerate, understand, or use effectively. So we have the results of tests, the questionnaires, the structured interviews, the experiments. We run our subjects through mazes, much as we run our rats, and we come up with "magic" numbers which we take to a chart and discover that something "significant" has been discovered.

In the material which follows, it is my intention to provide a "feeling" for the experience of youth. Intellectual explanations for behavior have an important place but can be overdone. We sometimes explain intellectually because it is too difficult for us to look, listen, and see emotionally.

We find it difficult to ask people to tell us about themselves. What we do is ask them to tell us how they feel about blacks, or sexuality, or how they feel about their mothers, brothers, fathers, or uncles. But we don't try to study them by asking them what really matters to them, or by setting the stage so that they can present us with this material in their own way.

This is not to say that case studies are not available. There are excellent ones. But there are also too many which are unnecessarily long, dull, overly scientific, pedantic, and highly structured. In studying such cases, we get so much information that we rarely know what it is that mattered to the person about whom the material was developed. People ought to be asked to tell us what they felt was important about their own experience in whatever way they want to present it. It doesn't seem particularly important how long, careful, complete, "scientific," or thorough such material is. What is important is that they be allowed to write or tell what really matters to them in their lives.

Many people were willing to tell me of some of their inner feelings. They seemed to be able to forget about psychological terms and scientific methods, although some had studied a bit of psychology, and to talk mainly about their feelings in words that have meaning to them and to other people.

The scientist will ask, and rightly so, about my population. My population comprised people between the ages of approximately seventeen and thirty-five. Some were students in good, solid colleges, in most cases doing adequate, and in many cases well above adequate academic work. I have more material to present on males than on females. Perhaps the reason for this is that inasmuch as I am a male, males found it easier to "let me in on their lives." Still, some women were able to do the same. These people were interested in many different areas of study—the arts, sciences, business, engineering, education.

My subjects were Catholics, Protestants, and Jews. Some were from wealthy families, others from poor families, still others from families at different levels throughout the range. Some were from the country and some from the city. Some had many brothers and sisters, and some were only children. Some had one or two siblings. Some probably had reasonably adequate parents and others had highly inadequate ones. Some subjects were quite bright, others far less bright. Most had intact homes, though a few did not. I have not provided this information for each person as I felt if it mattered to them, they would express it, and one of the tasks of the reader would be to try to understand their manner of doing this.

What I have to offer, with the permission of my students and patients, whose identities are carefully concealed and guarded, is a series of experiences and thoughts which have been very important in their development as they felt and saw it. In presenting the material, I have done nothing to it, with the exception of cutting sentences to protect anonymity. It is mainly the "feeling" for youth that I wish to convey to the reader. Youth, like any period of life, seems to be a period of struggle. They suffer, they feel, they fight to survive, they fail, they succeed, and they end up on many steps of the ladder between "succeeding" and "failing."

I have not been so presumptuous as to attempt to explain or interpret this material. My personal theoretical orientation is based upon psychoanalytic psychology, but I believe there are other methods of attempting to understand and develop a feeling toward human experience, and I believe that instructors and students have the right to choose their own way of doing this.

This is not my material; it belongs to my subjects. They were good enough to loan it to me. In my study of people in the college, clinic, and hospital situations and in practicing psychotherapy, I have learned something which "everyone" supposedly knows. They have taught me, and I thank them for doing it gently, that they are human beings, and we can be of more value to them if we look upon them not as cases, charts, numbers, correlations, labels, or parts of "controlled studies," but rather as people with thoughts, hopes, feelings, and anxieties, struggling to deal with themselves in what appears to be a very difficult world.

INTRODUCTION

Some things have changed since I edited *The Experience of Adolescence* seven years ago. For one thing, I no longer work in a university, but rather I divide my time between working in a large veterans' hospital, a private practice, and teaching medical and psychology students.

In this edition, entitled *The Experience of Young Adults*, I will leave untouched the sections that were most productive. I will also express as closely as possible the feelings of some Vietnam veterans who have been in individual or group therapy with me for the past six years. I have also added materials from other young people in great emotional pain as they related it to their therapist. The newer material is presented as Part I, the older as Part II.

S.J.G.

November, 1974
Wellfleet, Massachusetts

Dr. Stephen J. Golburgh received his A.B. degree from Boston University, his Ed. M. from Harvard University, and his Ed. D. from Boston University. He has taught at Boston University, Northeastern University, and Tufts University School of Medicine. He is interested primarily in individual and group psychotherapy based on psychoanalytically oriented principles.

Dr. Golburgh is a consultant to clinics, hospitals, and social service agencies. He has lectured extensively, particularly on psychotherapy. Presently he is Senior Staff Clinical Psychologist at the Boston V.A. Hospital, Clinical Assistant Professor of Psychiatry at Tufts University School of Medicine, and practices psychoanalytic therapy privately. Dr. Golburgh is best known for his psychotherapeutic work with young adults.

ALAN

"I have two children and want a husband. . . ."

I have known Alan, a Vietnam veteran, for six years. I see him once weekly in a psychotherapy group and once individually. He is 33 and what some would label schizophrenic. At times, he becomes so angry that to avoid hurting someone he goes into a catatonic stupor. He becomes mute, rigid, and feels terrified. He has been hospitalized seven times for this condition, remaining in the hospital only one or two days. To get him functioning, I, as his therapist, spend several hours sitting next to his bed telling him again and again that there is really nothing to fear, that his anger need not frighten him so. I stroke his shoulder often and tell him the truth—that I like him, care about him, am concerned about him, and promise over and over again that I will not desert or reject him. Alan at such times does not trust me fully, but gradually he starts to talk a little, telling me how angry he feels and how horribly frightened he is of his anger. He cries. He wonders how he can be a good father to his youngsters. At times he is so angry with them. His wife gives them so much and him so little, he feels. When he next mentions his wife he makes a slip of the tongue and says mother.

He wants so much to be mothered. He behaves in many ways like a young child, expecting and hoping that his wife will play mother to him. She does at times. When he is very upset she calls me and says angrily, "I have two children and want a husband, not a child." Yet, why did she marry him? She knew him for four years. Perhaps something about his childishness (sickness) appealed to some part of her. She does love him. They both know that.

She becomes angry at times and a psychiatric social worker is made available to her. She says she won't come to appointments, but she comes. Alan says of himself that he is no good, useless, not a man, perhaps a "queer." His childhood is one of almost total deprivation. He looks for mothers and fathers everywhere.

When the therapist told Alan of his coming vacation, Alan had a catatonic episode and needed two days of hospital care. "Please drive carefully," he said to the therapist. "How do I know you'll be back? You bastard, bitch, go fuck yourself, rotten Jew." The therapist listens and says nothing. After a few minutes the therapist tells Alan he will give him his summer address and telephone number: "Call me any time and I will talk with you or see you if need be." But those are just words to Alan. Of course, he could never trust anyone—why trust the therapist? But Alan is bright and he knows in a way that the therapist cares a great deal.

BILL SOMER

"Where do I fit in?"

Bill is rather special because he seems so healthy. Certainly he has his problems. He is too tied to his mother and at 23 he still sees himself as a kid. He is a very warm, likeable young man. Bill does well in school, has many and frequent significant relationships with women, and many male friends. He is very active. He is going somewhere and doing something all the time. His activities are generally worthwhile and people-oriented.

He is remarkably trustworthy and loyal. Highly responsible, there is little he could not be trusted with. A good athlete, he feels free with his body. He is quite well built, a bit short, and has a tendency to put on weight. He controls this with little difficulty. His parents love him fully and unconditionally. They both worked for years to send him to a boarding school as well as to college. He tells me he loves and respects them: "If I think something I'm going to do will upset them, I don't tell them." They give him his privacy, listen to him, trust him, and consider him as an adult person which, of course, he is.

But his father apparently is a passive man who has had difficulty earning a living. Bill, I think, is angry at his father. Why else do Bill and I have a relationship? I am many years older than he. Occasionally, I will ask Bill to do something for me and I always ask him if he would mind. Recently he remarked, "I can't say no when you ask me to do something." That worried me. Now I have my wife call him if we want anything done. I know it will make no difference. Incidentally, I pay him fairly for all he does for me. Bill smokes a little pot, has an occasional beer, loves his family, his car, his long hair, hockey, good food, women, money, and me.

What about mother? Does she hold on a bit, using guilt as a tool? Is she overly invested in him? I do not really know. His parents impress me as fine people. Bill is perhaps having the growing pains of his age. Perhaps I ameliorate these pains to some degree.

ANDREW

"A poorly handled transference situation"

Andrew was a good-looking, well-muscled 22-year-old when he first came to me for treatment. He was likeable, frightened, and seemed quite confused. Very unsure of himself, he behaved in an extremely passive manner over the several years that I saw him on a twice-a-week basis. Slowly his passivity became less and there was improvement in this area. In treatment he intellectualized continually. He had many fears—of the dark, of sexual thoughts, crowds, and death. He was terrified of expressing anger and would often tell me I behaved in such a manner as to make his getting angry at me impossible. I don't think I behaved in any particular fashion with Andrew. But perhaps he was right. I wonder about it.

He was quite seductive with me, with male teachers and male friends, yet he could not see this in himself. Therapy kept him from acting out his homosexual desires. Were he to have done so, he would only have felt more depressed, guilty, and childlike. He wanted so much to feel like a man. He was so fearful of working hard at treatment that I began to suspect an underlying severe paranoid condition. There were obvious paranoid trends.

Though basically heterosexual, Andrew was very upset over his homosexual feelings. Unconsiously he wanted to have a sexual experience with me, his therapist. He never verbalized this and probably was not aware of it. I never told him of it and perhaps I should have. I think so. He could not develop a "real" friendship with a girl. He had essentially a very meager sex life. He felt his penis was too small and he ejaculated very rapidly. This is considered by many to be a form of impotence. I agree that it is.

His problems with his parents were massive. Although he understood a great deal about himself, he was not free of his mother and had been further emotionally crippled by his weak, passive, cold, compliant father. He was very much a victim of his childhood and his feelings toward both parents and the way he was brought up. His dreams made it clear that he desired to play a passive role in a homosexual situation. He could not face interpretations pointing out the relationship between his conscious and unconscious anger and his homosexual feelings. He would listen to these interpretations, but he never seemed to be able to allow himself to feel them.

Our relationship seemed excellent. He never missed appointments, came on time, talked of his pain. I felt I understood him and could have helped him a great deal more. He showed what he felt was his anger to me, I believe, by "seeking a consultation," as he put it, with a very physically attractive, bright, and inexperienced therapist. It is customary, in most cases, for a consultant to discuss the patient with the original therapist, but I never received word of Andrew. Still, Andrew refers patients to me.

TOM

"My father used to lie in bed and beg for a drink."

Tom has been in individual therapy with me for over two years. He was seen for eight months previously by a therapist who left the area. Obviously, he will need many more years of treatment. He is so upset that even some improvement would be considered a very significant psychotherapy experience. Tom, a 25-year-old Vietnam veteran, first saw a psychologist over his fear that he was a homosexual because he was and, except for only occasionally, still is impotent with women. He had only one or two homosexual experiences, but he is most upset by homosexual urges that make him feel he is going to yell out, "I want to blow you." He becomes very guilty over these thoughts.

Homosexuality is only one of a large number of symptons. Very excessive use of alcohol is another. He is both anxious and depressed and cannot sleep unless he drinks himself into oblivion, always afraid of what might "slip out" when he talks. He is exquisitely sensitive to criticism, feels worthless, useless, and frequently considers suicide. Tom lives with his mother. His father has been dead for some time, an early death brought on by alcohol. In his last therapy session he reported that he was potent with a woman several times during a weekend when his mother was away.

Tom both hates and loves the memory of his father. He feels extremely guilty over this anger. He struggles in therapy to find positive things to say about the father and ignores the therapist when he interprets this. Mother sounds like an extremely controlling, domineering person who appears to be severely castrating. She has symbolically put Tom in the place of her husband and Tom has allowed this to happen. She will not let go of him nor does he, unconsciously, want to give her up. She criticizes every girl be becomes involved with.

Tom comes from a lower class background. He sees the therapist as an all-good father/mother figure. He shows hostility by missing appointments and making disparaging remarks about the therapist. Basically, the therapeutic alliance is excellent even though Tom is a so-called "acter outer." He is quite open with the therapist and a good deal of material is coming out into the open in a usable fashion. He understands the concept of projection and is able to see and control his feelings that people hate him or are looking at him. These understandings are conscious and emotional. Tom has been able to act on them to a limited degree up to the present time. It is foreseen that he will make greater strides as time passes.

His desperation is terrifying to the listener. Tom knows what happens to alcoholics as time passes. He also sadly looks at me as he asks, "Can we do it?" I tell him the truth, that we can do it but that he must follow the rules and talk about whatever comes to mind. He tells me he is afraid of doing this, as his hand shakes nervously to get the fifth cigarette that hour. I say, "I have no plans of leaving you, Tom." He looks up, breathes deeply, and relaxes. "I'm so tired all the time. I can't sleep unless I'm very drunk."

What are you afraid will happen if you let go, relax? Perhaps you're afraid of your dreams? What do you think?"

"I can't tell you my dreams."

"I know it's hard, but you can tell me. Go ahead. You'll feel better."

"It's always the same dream. [Long pause] I'm fucking my mother."

"That's not an uncommon dream. Let's study it and try to understand it. Tell me more."

JERRY

"I'm getting better maybe."

Doctor, it's always been hell, a kind of hell you can't understand no matter how experienced or well trained you are. They shipped me off to boarding school when I was four. Believe it or not, I knew even then I was gay. In many years of analysis I have not told my analyst that. I realized it clearly when I was 15 or a bit younger. I never felt well. I still almost never do. I still go to my analyst. He keeps me going. He, my wife, and a friend I have known for many years. I think of him as my final saviour if I finally fall apart. Often it's an hour-by-hour fight.

The depression makes it hard to move my body. I don't want to talk. I don't want people to see me. I don't want to work. I don't want to do anything but sleep. By the way, I'm successful at what I do. I earn a very adequate income and I have a fine reputation. It means shit to me. In fact, I am excellent at my work. I do love my kids. I also love my wife very much. She loves me too, but in a different way. She's much healthier than I. I need her like I need my analyst and she knows it. The homosexual urge tortures me. There was a short period when it seemed to be gone, but it came back stronger than ever. Now I want to act it out. I am going to. I don't give a damn. I've got to get it out of my system. I know it won't help. Fuck my analyst. By the way, I love him. He's a god to me. He has almost complete control over me. He is a very straight, honest, human caring man. He pretends to be hard-boiled, but underneath he's soft, warm, sweet, and loving. He's also crazy. He even knows it, but it's an OK kind of craziness.

My wife uses me. She doesn't even know it. In other ways she's very good to me. She has really hurt me at times, less so at other times. She thinks she knows more than she does. She's hung up with her father and she's a little girl at times. She's stubborn, wants her way, and usually gets it. She knows I'm gay. She denies it, but she's not stupid. I can perform meaningfully with her if the conditions are just right. But then there's the kids' bath, or time to fold the laundry. She's a good woman. She promised me she would never leave me. She never will. I won't let her. I'm smarter than she and she knows that, too. I don't usually use it on her. I'm getting better maybe. It's so long and so up and down. Good periods are so few, but it feels like they are going to come more frequently.

MRS. HANOVER

"I'll forgive but I'll never forget."

Doctor, I never really should have married. I'm too childlike and unstable. I have been since I was a youngster. I can't really help it, but I think only of myself. My comforts, my joys. Things have to go my way all the time. The world owes me something. Yes, I know this is foolish but I still feel and act this way. Then I get paranoid. I think the family is taking me for a ride. I put the money in the checking account. I do what they want. It's never really what I want. Of course, I never really know what I want. I feel as if I've been trained by my husband. He's not well and is unable to work. That really is true. He tells me what to do and I do it. He gave me a pretty bad time a little while ago. He hit where it hurt most. He hit hard. Maybe it was right. Maybe he should have done what he did. He made me feel abandoned.

I don't always think the way I do now. It's just that right now I'd really like to be free. Free of my physically sick husband and kids and coping and adjusting. I'd like to go my own way. Be done with them once and for all. Of course, I have no place to go. No place I really want to go. My husband has the ability to entertain the fantasy that he understands me. Before he got sick he was a practicing therapist. He was very good. He probably could be again. He said if anyone could help me, you could. He knows the people in the field very well.

Anyway, he doesn't understand me very much at all. Yes, at times I guess I have to build a life of my own. Sort of consider my marriage a job and build something outside of it just for me. My mother always said, "I'll forgive but I'll never forget." I'm afraid I'm that way, too. But I don't know what I will not forget. People seem to appreciate very little. I include myself. It's almost like the more you do or give, the more they expect from you. Like my mother, I can never please him. Oh yes, occasionally, for a minute or two. It's like he's doing me a big favor.

There is really nothing I can do about it. I need him and love him. We are very formal with each other these days. Quite polite and proper. I guess that results from you and his therapist. You who manipulate lives when you really don't know the whole story. You never could. Life has no meaning for me. It's massive confusion. I don't get the support I need. I'm very good at my work and it's very important work, but I often wonder if I really am as sincere as I think I am. I do think I am.

I've always wanted to write. I feel I can. I've done some writing and it's been published. But to earn a living, and God knows I must do that, is another story. I smoke too much. I know I'm working well when I smoke a lot. My smoking also sickens me. I'm afraid of suicide, but you don't need to worry. I know you're not supposed to care, but you probably do. My husband used to care a great deal. Like the song, "Tired of living, scared of dying." That's me. I have developed the fine capacity to feel profoundly worried for myself. I know. We need to explore my past—for many years. That's how it works. I'll go along. I don't give up easily, Doctor. I'm really quite bright, as by now I assume you know. I'm also quite hostile. I assume you know this too.

Tell me. Are you listening to me? My husband rarely does. He pretends. You probably do the same thing. I don't like men very much. Don't you get bored just listening? You rarely say a word. But as I talk to you I feel stronger. It burns off the anger some. It feels constructive. Feeling so depressed and angry makes it easier for me to write. And I think I have a lot to say. It's probably the same nothing that everyone says who thinks she has a lot to say—or never bothers trying to say because she knows she really hasn't got anything to say. How much time do we have left, Doctor? Oh, 20 minutes.

MR. YOUNG

"Today the whole idea seems ridiculous to me."

It was a very strange experience visiting a gay bar again. "Why so?" the psychologist asked. The twenty-nine-year-old lawyer tensed slightly. He had been married for four years to an interesting, bright, and understanding wife, and they had a two-year-old child. He was studying legal medicine, which includes psychiatric problems. He had undergone pyschotherapeutic treatment for "homosexual interests," among other things, and considered the results successful. The opportunity to speak with this young man resulted from my academic work with people in training in the psychological sciences.

"I was just plain queer when I was nineteen. Today the whole idea seems ridiculous to me. I'm very much involved with my wife, love her, and am quite happy sexually with her. I'll tell you the story in short form because otherwise it would take years. I met my wife when I was twenty and my therapist when I was twenty-one. I got married at twenty-two. I learned certain things from my therapist that essentially changed my life. Homosexual activity calmed me down, I thought. It was like a drug. I felt I needed it, but it only made me more fearful, more tense, and more depressed. I had the dream that my partner really accepted me fully. I got very little kick out of sex. It was the physical closeness that mattered.

"In a way I was showing my father what a lousy job he had done. In my homosexual activity I often played the role of the good father. I behaved toward my partner as I wished my father had behaved toward me. Also, behaving homosexually made me feel that men wanted me, which really meant to me that Father wanted me. Father didn't. The men did. I'm good-looking. They wanted to use me. I wanted to be 'fathered.' I was terrified of women. I felt they would hurt me as my mother had. I know this sounds simple, but it was hard to really learn it and

13

act on it. My homosexual relationships never lasted very long, but I was afraid of getting close to a woman.

"Paul, my lover when I was acting homosexually, and I talked a lot about our 'real' relationship, but we were kidding ourselves and each other. We were always using each other. We didn't really even like each other. Isn't it ridiculously crazy? We were very quick to show our deeply hidden hate by annoying each other, setting traps to catch each other with someone else. We both promised to be faithful, but those are just words. Occasionally, I noticed he behaved a bit sadistically toward me in a sexual and physical way.

"I'm not a scientist or a psychologist, Doctor, but I know a great deal about homosexuals. Many relationships are similar to the one I just described. Most are worse and plenty are just plain psychotic. Many homosexuals, as you know, are terrified of treatment and some pick a 'gay' therapist who is not competent. Im not saying that a gay therapist cannot be competent if he's well-trained and has been working on his problems with his own therapist so that he doesn't foul up the treatment for his patient. You see, Doctor, forming a 'relationship' with a woman is, I think, more complicated and fulfilling than it is with a man. Because women are more complicated, they require an adult emotionally. So-called 'homosexuals' are, I think, children. All you need do is watch them behave for a while. Of course, I may be wrong.

"Doctor, I think what I'm saying is basically true. The sample may be biased, but I don't think so because I knew hundreds. For example, the friends of my friends who have other friends. Very often they had gone to boarding school, were very attractive, came from broken or chaotic homes, had weak or very cruel fathers. Most of all, it's the situation with the mother. It can take many forms, but it's always castrating and destructive. Mother is a combination of things, or fewer are very strange in only one way. Mother was unloving and ungiving from early in life. Her parents usually had or have sex problems. Mother throws herself at the male child in her seductiveness. She makes him guilty over everything. She wants to control and manipulate him. She doesn't want to give him up to another woman. Sometimes she'll actually say so. I see many very lonely 'homosexual' people, people who drink too much and, more recently, who use drugs, people who really don't feel accepted. They say they do, but it's crap. They know they are kidding themselves. Many of them are excellent con men and they con each other and themselves often, and most of the time they don't know it.

"They are always afraid of age and growing older. They believe age makes them less desirable. This is not at all necessarily so. They are like frightened children, terrified that they will not be desired. Some have little to offer except their bodies. The others are too afraid to offer anything but their bodies. In treatment I learned that people do and can change. I saw myself changing in many ways, but only very slowly. Anger had always been the major problem for me. I could not express it properly. Holding it in made me tense, shaky, and hurt. It caused panic attacks that at times were so bad I could barely work. My mother and father were very upset people. Father was a good guy but weak. Mother was mean, depressed, and should never have married. She wanted a little girl and I was rejected from birth. She could not love me and slowly I learned I could not expect from her what she never had given and didn't have to give.

"For a long time I looked for something that didn't and doesn't exist. Many things, in fact, First, I'd say a father. Really I suppose the father I needed so badly as a child and never had. In my imagination I used to think I'd find him in a gay bar or on a street corner or in a men's room. It's been said that inside every homosexual there is a heterosexual hammering to get out. I believe that. What do you think? It's what you think that matters [softly]. I still get anxious around 'homosexuals', whatever that means. The homosexual urges don't haunt me any more. I'm really too busy to be bothered and too involved with my wife and child."

MR. WALSH

"I had regressed into very early childhood."

It was August and my therapist was as usual on vacation. He is a very kind but firm man. I know where he goes to vacation and I can call him, but I don't. July had been literally hell. I felt I would have to be hospitalized at any moment. I had regressed into very early childhood. I decided to vacation the entire month of August. He had taken two weeks. We arranged telephone sessions for the last two weeks of August.

Today was the day. I had a 7:50 A.M. appointment. I awoke at six. Getting to sleep the night before was hell. At 6 A.M. I shaved, showered, dressed, and sat near the phone. I guess I wondered if he would be there. Perhaps he had died? The dependence is so great, as it needs to be at times in deep therapy. I had diarrhea. My hands were shaking. I knew that when I heard his voice I would settle down. I was afraid the phone would go out of order. Were the clocks in the house set right? Perhaps he had died. The wish beneath the irrational fear? No.

I didn't want to be alone. It was 7:30 A.M. My wife was feeding the kids. "Susie," I called, "stay with me." I paced nervously near the phone. Suppose I had to have a bowel movement in the middle of the session? I have a bathroom, yet I'm so frightened. I have a problem with bowel movements. Nothing physical. Fine physicians have examined me and stated this clearly. But I have to have what I call a "good" movement every morning. If I don't have it I'm in for a pretty tough day. But I've gotten off the track.

At 7:40 I made the call. The answering service answered. The psychologist was with another patient. I would have to wait. I sat on the couch, nervously smoking one cigarette after another. There was so much to say. I had thought of writing notes, but I knew he didn't want my notes but rather what passed through my mind. I called again. He answered. I said, "Go fuck yourself." He said "yes." I told him so many things in that forty-five minute session. I felt so much better. He is both my "good" mother and my "good" father. I wondered a little if perhaps after so many years I was not seeing real results from my psychotherapy.

He always asks "Why?" It's hard to answer. I often don't know. Sometimes I do a little. Sometimes I made up a story to tell him. I take pleasure in telling him a story that will please him. I like to get him to smile. I want to get him to give me something, some magic. I know he hasn't got it to give. No therapist has. Every patient wants it. I'm stubborn. I'm still demanding it from him. He says nothing. He'll occasionally say, "You want to believe in magic." The session went very well. I look forward to tomorrow morning.

MRS. JORDAN

"A difficult situation"

I am a patient. I have suffered from what I consider severe depression for many years. I am twenty-nine, married to a successful lawyer, and have one little boy. I have been to many doctors and none has really helped me. My first psychiatrist was young. I later found I was his first private patient. I also later found out that he had serious problems of his own. He helped me a great deal, though. I saw him for about eight years on a twice-a-week basis. He was supportive, encouraging, practical, and warm. I liked him in a sincerely human way.

I finally realized he could not help my depression. I could not tell him or break off therapy with him. I liked him too much. My husband did not like him because he knew the doctor did not understand me. Finally, after two years, I asked to get another opinion as to my treatment. I was sent to a woman psychologist who I liked and who suggested I needed deeper treatment. By deeper treatment she meant therapy based primarily on the work of Freud. This work is done by psychiatrists, psychologists, and some lay people who have undergone rigorous training. The most important thing in their training is their own personal psychotherapy.

Doctor, my next therapist was older and more businesslike. He never called me by my first name but always Mrs. Jordan. Eight years have passed and I continue to see this therapist three times a week. I lie on a couch and talk about whatever comes to mind. At least, I try to. I listen to what I say and we slowly work to put it together. The funny thing is I have to do almost all the work myself. My psychologist is excellent. He says very little.

I have learned a great deal about myself and treatment has been very painful. My husband has been basically helpful. Sometimes he doesn't really know what to do, but his intuition is good.

Slowly I am getting better, but progress is so slow that I very often get discouraged and feel even more depressed. But one cannot expect to change many years of a particular style of life in a short time. Good therapy takes much time in order that the earlier childhood problems can be understood and studied, resulting in a more complete and fulfilling life. After they are "worked through," the problems can be resolved. It took a long time to really trust my therapist. Perhaps at times I don't trust him even now. He has never given me any reason to distrust him. Actually, he's a very nice person.

I have learned some of the factors that cause my depression. I have learned, in fact, that depression is just a word to indicate that there are very strong inner feelings and conflicts going on. I have learned that I am basically angry at my childhood, my mother and father, and the way I was brought up. I am afraid of my own anger. I am afraid to live in the present, so I withdraw from it by taking all kinds of pills that don't help. Perhaps I'll go to sleep. Or I'll cop out by actually feeling exhausted. I am often terribly childish and make mountains out of molehills. I act like a little girl at times. I would rather, on one level, live in a world of fantasy than actually face reality and fight with it like an independent, free, creative adult. I am working on it, though, and there are some better periods from time to time.

Working at it is hard as hell. You sometimes feel it's mainly a question of getting from one hour through to the next. I learned I must force myself to be more active physically and mentally. I have learned to be more careful of my diet. I am less angry. Still very angry, yes, but not quite the same. I have a great many fears. None of them are realistic, but this does not make them any less terrifying or upsetting. I now have better control over these fears in general, although there are certain very difficult periods. It is during these periods that I need my husband most.

A YOUNG MAN MEETS HIS FAMILY AFTER TEN YEARS

"Mother is still important"

Doctor, we decided, my wife and I, to spend a month together on vacation as you have so often suggested. It was a remarkable experience. I met my wife and children. I worked long hours. I was usually asleep when they went to school and when I got home they were asleep. I saw them a little on Saturdays—very little—and a little on Sundays. I was so depressed I slept most of Sunday. In our years of marriage, I knew my wife only very little and my children even less. I learned so much during that month that I am shocked, confused, amazed, and pleased.

My God. My wife is a real person. I thought I was the only person in the world. She has feelings, fears, great strengths. She is a magnificent young woman whom I have shit on for years. I'm lucky she's a little nuts or she would have left me long ago. Doctor, I learned she even had problems. Real honest to God problems. Problems that hurt her. She has been in treatment for a year, but I took it as a joke. You know, it's fashionable. Besides, I can afford it. But she must continue to see that therapist and she knows it and I don't think she knows this, but I know she needs to continue. She will.

So will I. Hell, I find I can still learn. Learn to really deeply care about another human being. I never have before. But now I know I do. It frightens me. I just want to sit and talk to her all the time. I have realized that the kids need her too. God. I'm lucky if I get thirty minutes of attention in a day. I look forward to it. I'll do anything for it. Probably rob, destroy, perhaps even myself, in order to get it. Don't get upset, Doctor. You're next in the line of importance. But she could overturn you in a minute and you mean a tremendous amount to me. You know that.

I am really in love with this woman. I would die for her and I'm terrified of death. I would steal to please her, and I may even get well for her. She is suddenly the most important thing in the world to me. And now she is truly more important to me than Mother. Mother is still important. I'm sorry to say it. I wish to God I could get more fully away from her, but it feels like she's pulling on me and I feel for a moment I really love her. I don't really love her, I hate and loathe her, but now and then I feel I love her. It's very strange. I hate her so, I can taste it. Why won't she die? Die, you bitch. I'm angry right now.

We have a dog. My sons love this dog and we have some moderately severe problems with the dog. My wife pays a great deal of attention to this dog. You see, she is as "hung up" with the fuckin', crazy, neurotic, pissing dog as my sons. Seriously, we probably should reasonably get rid of the dog, but I had a dog I loved when I was a kid. You can't imagine what that dog meant to me. That dog was a "problem" also. To my mother. Solution: fuck me and the dog went. One of the many things from Mother I'll never forget. Bitch, rat, goddamn disease.

So, our dog stays. We'll fight it through no matter what. I won't do to my kids what she did to me. Maybe she didn't mean to rip me apart. I don't know. I can't believe she meant to hurt me so terribly. What do you think? "What matters is what you think, but I think she knew more about what she was doing than you are willing to admit to yourself. Go on with your thoughts." Wait a minute, Doctor, it hurts, you know. Well, my sons. They are beautiful, bright, alert, alive. All my kids are. But I'll tell you about my youngest son as an example. I hope that doesn't mean I care less about my daughter. She is remarkable.

My son needs a father. I have begun to be one. We both like it. He's a charming kid because my wife was able to arrange things so that he was not destroyed by me and my illness. He has some problems, but to a reasonable degree I'll be able to help him out now. I'll never be able to undo the damage I did, but the truth is I didn't do much damage. I did only a fair job. Now I can do a good job. It's going to be hard for me because I find it very hard to discipline him. I can't easily punish him physically. "Are you afraid he won't like you?" Yes, terrified.

Anyway, this kid is very "neat," as the kids say today. He is a real live person with ideas and some fears and hopes and worries. He is growing up and I now see it. I believe he idolizes me. I idolize him. I'm worried about him. He says he wants to be a veterinarian. Surer than hell I believe he means it. I know many kids want to be veterinarians as they go through certain stages, but with my kids it seems different. Of course, every parent says "with my kids it's different" and it almost never is, but with my kids it is.

My older daughter wants to be a veterinarian, too. She's got a little of me in her. She's oversensitive and a bit moody. But she is as sharp as hell. She knows me better than I know her. She's wild about me. I adore her. She's very beautiful and she's sweet and earthy and human and she wants to be kind to me and animals and fish. We can talk together like two grown-up people. I hate to be alone. She can babysit for me. My wife sometimes arranges for my little daughter to babysit for me. We talk about everything under the sun. I tell her how much I love her. She laughs and says, "Daddy, I know that." I always told her I loved her when I was acting crazy and yelling and behaving like a child. I told my sons also. When they were or are asleep at night I sneak into their rooms and hold them and think how lucky I am. Tears come to my eyes. This still happens almost every night. I don't know if my wife knows about it.

And then there is Carl. I've known him since I was born. He is the whole world to me. I admire and respect him. He is a competent teacher, a fine administrator, and fair-to-good in some other work he does. But he's a really fine human being. Yes, he has his problems. He's pretty angry inside, overly secretive, and he finds it hard to let go. He thinks he has had a secret from me for over thirty years, but I have known the "secret" since I was twelve and I never mentioned it to him. I will very soon.

If he needed money I would give it to him without question. I like his wife very much. She's funny and bright and often high. She, like all people, also has problems. I hated her when I met her. She was taking him away from me. She did. But she knew that for many subtle reasons she and I must learn to live together. Carl is very important to me and I am very important to him also. We really do care about each other and like each other. We respect each other. I can be very free with her and she with me. She is totally honest and direct. Like my wife. She is a fine person. She has many interests, she is funny, talented artistically, and very attractive. "If you can't beat them, join them." Maybe we both, his wife and I, felt the same way. I don't know.

Carl is practical, level-headed, strong, well controlled, and quiet. Carl is truly trustworthy, honest, and loyal. He seems to be getting more intelligent as each year passes. I am far brighter than he. I earn more money, but he is in better control of his life. At least I think so. My wife and his are good friends. It is indeed a beautiful relationship. No. We don't all sleep together. No, we don't swap wives.

My wife just spends money. You see, we have a joint checking account. I make deposits and she writes checks and checks and checks. Really, she's not too bad. Once in a while she seriously gets too friendly with that checkbook, but compared to so many others she's pretty good.

She wants very much to help me, but I often interpret some of the things she does as totally selfish. I'm still not convinced. I guess I was brought up to believe you can't trust anyone. Really I do trust her, but every now and then I get the feeling she might be using me and thinking of leaving me. By the way, she isn't doing either. These are just feelings I get, but they are tremendously powerful. Often, or rather usually, my wife picks just the right moment to ask for something. The rare moments when I'm in a good mood. She spots them and uses them. But, you see, she doesn't use them to her advantage, but to our advantage. I can't believe this but it is clearly true.

We have a lousy sex life. I've had many sexual problems, as you know, and I'm really lousy in bed. She's a fairly normal young woman. I'm doing a bit better lately, but she's been pretty mad at me underneath for a long time. I can do better as I get to understand myself better by talking with you, Doctor. And by arranging my time better. Like don't take a sleeping pill at night when your wife is in the bathtub. Or several sleeping pills which you think you need but know you really don't. Doctor, my wife and I have to get to know each other better both emotionally and physically. We're working at it. I know what I'm saying is childish, but it's practical. She has to be more active sexually because I guess I'm scared of being active. She has to get me interested. What do you think? Why don't you tell her this? "Go ahead with your thoughts." Christ, I'll be a therapist before I'm through here. When do I get my diploma? "When you deserve it. I want to know your thoughts. Some of what you are asking about represents resistance. What might you be avoiding?"

By the way, her parents are great. It's almost like they are my parents too. I'm deeply fond of them. Especially my father-in-law. He's really nuts, but he is also most amazing. He's cheap as hell, brilliant, and strong and practical. He's ruled by his mother whom he hates but believes he loves. But he's a very fine person. He, my therapist, Carl, and my wife are the only ones who can give me hell and I'll take it. It's strange to let your father-in-law blast you. But I let him. I like to think he does it for my own good, but he probably does it for his daughter's sake. He doesn't really care about me. Or does he? I don't know. Hell, he might. My wife just went out. I am very mad at you for leaving me. I can't take it. I am afraid the kids will get hurt. The dog is bugging me out of my mind. Please talk to me about these things. Why is there an extra heart worm pill out? Did you forget yesterday? Why don't you listen to me?

I'm very angry. I cannot babysit for the dog and have a sitter for kids. The kids are outside. I'm stuck inside with the dog barking and running. I'm very mad. No sitter for tonight. I screamed at Mark. I think I'm going crazy. I can't work. The dog is racing around. We are not going out tonight. I am going to think more of what's best for me from now on. I lunged at Mark because he opened the door and let the dog out. I'm so angry. I had to get the hunk of dog meat back. I called you, Doctor, at 10:30. You said, "go for a walk." I can't. I'm baby-sitting for the dog. You are taking advantage of me.

All the sitters and calls are expensive. It's getting crazy. I need liquor or dope or sleep. Afraid to sleep. Dog will kill me. I'm a no good rotten bastard. Very scared. I don't care any more. Suicide might be best. I haven't got the guts. I'm tired of living this way and afraid of change. You are a child. You forget the most important thing—*ME*. I'll try to be cool. You use me terribly. I'm so weak. I'm finished now. All control is gone. I want to break and destroy. I still love you very much. I would do anything for you. Why do you torture me? I know we need the dog. For the boys, but he overguards and gets me uptight. If my father were alive he could help. Would you please call my mother today or Tuesday or Wednesday or Thursday for three minutes. You don't have to, but it would mean a lot to me. Again, you don't have to. I find myself relaxing a little. It's eleven now. I figure you will be home at one. That means two hours. I'm going to "take a hit." I'm terrified of this loneliness. Not going out tonight is not to hurt you but because David has no one to sit in his place and I need to relax. It's been pretty wild here.

I'm afraid I'm going to die. The dog is quiet now. Standing on a chair watching the kids. I'm hungry. It's eleven. I have to make something for myself. I'm out of cigarettes. I just looked again. I'll send the sitter and kids to the store. I did. The dog is going wild again. He sees the kids leaving. I'm yelling at him. It helps. This is foolish. Needing cigarettes so badly but I'm so mad. At twelve I'll have a vodka and tonic. I'm going to get some grass to smoke. I will die soon and you will be sorry. That sounds foolish, I realize. I have the vodka with orange juice because I won't make lunch for myself. I'm not a horse or a dog to be trained as you are trying to do. Now I've made you recently feel you're all right about everything, but you're not and you know it. But it doesn't matter. I'm going to get stoned now.

Now I went to the bathroom to piss, but I didn't have to piss. I got stoned. Where is the dumb babysitter with my cigarettes? I need one. Soon vodka and orange juice. Only three-quarters of an hour. The dog has relaxed and is sitting quietly. I feel a little better, but I can't wait for the vodka and orange juice. I'll get it now. Make the drink. Thank God it is quiet here now. The dog is lying at my feet resting. I'm drinking vodka. Where are the cigarettes? The kids have not returned. Stupid kid. But he has my kids. We're trying, but it's awfully painful. Christ, this is quite a note. I wonder if I could make a good living writing. Probably not. It's 11:30. Vodka and orange juice finished. I feel I need to wash my face. Where is the kid with the cigarettes? The dog is on guard again. He needs to run and fuck. As a neighbor said, he doesn't lead a normal life. Face-washing time again.

I guess I would rather smoke than protect myself against lung cancer or a coronary or emphysema. I've seen these things and they are pretty bad. Face-washing time. I washed my face and looked for cigarettes. None. But there is a butt that has one drag on it. Maybe two. Two drags. It was wonderful. Maybe one more drag. Yes. I got it. Still looks like another. Yes, I got it. Still one more. Yes. I got it. Maybe another yet. I got it but that is the end. I'll go look again. Where is the stupid baby-sitter and my kids and my cigarettes? I gave the bastard one dollar and told him to keep the change. I'm really getting hungry. Wait. No cigarettes. I'm heating up a frozen chicken pie. It's twenty before noon. It takes forty-five minutes. 12:30 it should be done. At twelve I've got to take my pills. I'll get them ready, wait. I just took my pills. I didn't take another of the pills. I took too much this morning. I'm OK.

Where is the kid with the cigarettes? I have to check the stove. Wait. Stove is groovy. Still no cigarettes. But I found another butt. Maybe three drags. Where is the kid with my kids? I worry too much about the kids. Light the other butt. It's good—soothing. I'm psychotic now. Dog is on guard again. He could and would kill anyone that tried to hurt us. How could you leave me without cigarettes? I'll look again. No. This hasn't happened for many years. Where is the kid with my kids and the cigarettes. Soon, they will be here. The dog is resting now. It is quiet. I'm hungry. Thirty minutes to go before the chicken pie is ready. That can be a long time, yet sometimes it's nothing.

What if I fall asleep with the chicken pie in the oven? It may burn the place and me and the dog to hell. I think I need another vodka and this time some low calorie drink. I want to get some sleep without knocking myself to death with pills. I'm going to get the vodka. Wait.

I started the second vodka. I make big drinks. No sitter, no kids, crazy dog, no cigarettes, no wife. I want to fall asleep but I'm worried about the oven cooking—overcooking the chicken pie. It's 12:10. Twenty minutes can be a long time. The kids need lunch. Is there any food here for me to make? Wait. Yes, plenty of food. I'll have to put the dog in his cage because the baby-sitter is afraid of him. He barks. Still no sitter. Too dumb to know I needed a cigarette bad. Fuckin' kid. Fuckin' world. Born to die. I think Pope John said, "Any day is a good day to die or to be born." I liked him.

It's now 12:15. At 12:30 the chicken pie is finished, I hope. But where are the kids, the cigarettes, and the sitter? Weird kid, I guess. Soon I will sleep. In death, yes, but I will not die yet. Hell, there is the chicken pie and the cigarettes and eventually you'll come home. And you're going to get it. For nothing, I know. Time to check the pie and look out the window for the kids. I'll call Mother. Please understand. I'm crying now. Check the pie first.

Here is the sitter, the kids, and the cigarettes. Thank God. He'll feed the kids. I'll supervise. The kid won't talk. I need a sitter for tonight. David has a previous engagement. I tried to con him, but I couldn't. He has a sister. She's nine or ten. No. We're stuck home. But lots of cigarettes. Thank heaven. It's 12:30. You should be home soon. I've got to really supervise. David is not much of a cook. I had to make lunch. David couldn't get it together. I just fired him. My wife is back. I'm a prick. But you still don't understand. You never will because you're really not bright enough.

MY HUSBAND

"He was a most peculiar man."

Very few people really knew my husband, Doctor. He was a most peculiar man. His life had always been hell and joy. He was a fine therapist, the very best, everyone knew that. He always said he would die young; he had what he called a "predilection to death." He did not want to die. He had a great deal to do in living. He loved me in a most unusual way. Very deeply in all ways. I felt similarly toward him, only more so. I always knew that I came first even though it seemed as if the patients were his entire life. Nowhere else was he really as happy as he was in the consulting room. Here he could practice his skill and his art and feel and know he was easing the pain, even if only for a little while.

He had the best training and studied with the leaders in psychotherapy. Every patient was a joy to him. He never gave up. If things were not going well he would ponder and ponder and try to get movement and growth going again. Doctor, you know he felt he failed with only one patient and, truthfully, I've been a therapist myself long enough to know he didn't. But he felt he failed and he tortured himself.

He learned that "life is change. If there is no change, there is death." He felt life must move and people must create because "life constantly was moving." He thought about his patients constantly and truly loved all of them. There were so many because he could rarely say "no" to a person. But each was unique to him. Someone very special. I must admit he did have two or three favorites. I resented very rarely the love, loyalty, and devotion he gave to his patients. Fees meant little to him. To cushion the pain of young adults with mangled childhoods was all he cared about.

To "get it out and look at it," he would say, will really help them. But "getting it out" the correct way is hard and so he worked like a demon. He was gentle, a true craftsman. With him, treatment was long. He would not do a patchwork job. He had to give all he had and even more. And he did. He will always be remembered by most patients he treated. His honesty, warmth, caution, and sincere concern. They felt it. You could feel it emanate from him when you were with him. He was no different when doing therapy than he was at any other time. He was never a phony.

Our children loved him. I don't think they were jealous of the patients. He happily found time for them. It wasn't the amount of time, but what went into it. He always put everything into everything he did. His was a fully and creatively lived life. Doctor, I feel strange. Talking of my dead husband, who was the finest of psychologists, to another psychologist.

Yes, he had his problems. He worked too hard, had problems with his mother for many years, and occasionally worried about molehills. He was treated successfully by one of the finest men around. Treatment did wonders for him. And so he practiced what he believed in. And it almost always worked for him. "Sometimes some people need more time," he would say. He was almost always right. He thought badly of the therapists who saw their patients for three or four years and then got bored with them and threw them out. He always said, "People need lots of time to grow up."

He became a health food addict because his therapist had been. He struggled all his life with smoking. He went back for further treatment to deal with this symptom, but "the old man," his therapist, was long gone and he never really wanted to see anyone else. His philosophy was "don't change horses in the middle of the race" and I think he was generally right. People used to come to him for treatment because they were upset about this or that in their present treatment. He always listened carefully and thought deeply. He usually sent the patient back to the original therapist. If the therapist was in need of help, he would talk the patient over with the therapist. This was very time-consuming and he never charged enough for it. Oh, he always charged a standard fee, but money was his least concern. He was far from perfect. Very far, and we knew it together. He was obsessed with cleanliness, appearing correctly and behaving properly. He became, as he grew older, a typical New England Yankee.

During the earlier part of our marriage I was the controlling figure, but that stopped. We became the central figures. To please me was to please himself, and if I could please him it would please me. I wish I could have gotten those cigarettes away from him. We both knew what he was doing to himself. Yes, he had trouble with alcohol for a while and then he "abused" sedatives, stimulants, very powerful ones for many years. He was not a drug addict, but he and I had a rough time then. Getting off the drugs was the hardest part of our marriage for me. I really could do very little for him except be there. There were some things I went along with that I didn't like, but I never said anything about it. He knew I knew. It helped him and he appreciated it greatly.

He always said, "When I die who will take care of my patients?" He made very careful arrangements for that. He selected who he felt was the best psychologist for each of his patients and left a note for me to inform them. He had a quiet wit and subtle sense of humor. He was very loose, open, and honest. He was very human. His anger was never very real or strong and it passed in seconds. He loved and idolized his children and they felt and still feel similarly about him.

THE LITTLE
DOCTOR

"Dr. Nador—A very gentle man"

Doctor, it's a very hard story to tell because it's lasted about forty years. He's a short man, he has always had trouble with his weight. He's a fine man. He reminds me of the song, "To Know Him Is to Love Him." I was seven years old and woke up with a high fever at 3:00 A.M. There was a snowstorm raging outside. My mother wanted the doctor. "I hope I didn't wake you, Doctor," mother would say. Of course she didn't. He was catching up on the latest developments in trout fishing. Funny thing, though, he always answered, "No, I've been doing some late reading." At 3:00 A. M.!

Well, let me tell you about that night. This fifty-year-old man couldn't get his car out of the driveway. So he walked, carrying a heavy medical bag in the snow up a large hill to where we lived. I had a bad sore throat and in those days there were no wonder drugs. Anyway, it hurt, but I was mainly scared. So the physician treated my by teaching me to play poker, giving me some aspirin, and giving me a chance to settle down. By playing poker with me, he told me he liked me and cared about me. He told me, without one word, that I could depend on him and trust him. He in a sense gave me permission to ignore an hysterical, overly terrified, unconsciously hostile mother and a consciously angry, confused father who tried but didn't know how. No, his English isn't excellent and he hadn't graduated from one of the so-called "good" medical schools.

You see, he came to this country when he was a youngster. Alone. He had no one here. He had to eat, so he had to work. He also went to school. When did he sleep? And it went on and on. Through medical school, which got screwed up by the First World War, and after medical school, while taking advanced study in a hospital that still exists. My God, it still exists. He visited it last month after fifty years. He studied by candlelight, he ate some funny kind of fish because it was all he could afford. He retired a while ago, but you know he's still there. He's always been there. When no one else was, at least for me. Perhaps without him I would have become psychotic.

He was the only person, as I was growing up, who told me he had faith in me, that I was worthwhile, and could be liked and perhaps even loved. He was and is an amazing man. When I was in college I took a course in psychological testing. There was a very complicated test we had to learn and practice giving. I'd decided he really wasn't very bright. After all, he had an accent and he hadn't studied at Harvard, and he didn't have a fancy office or a nurse or secretary. Some people would call him second-rate. But that's because they never really knew him. And they didn't know that his I.Q. was 154 (about as high as you can go), and he reads medical journals every day and night, and he took advanced courses just about anywhere they were offered, and he never missed a medical lecture or meeting unless he was called away to take care of a patient. You see, the patient always came first with him. And if he was unsure of something about a patient, he would call in the area's leading specialist. And they came fast for this old man.

Incidentally, his son is a "specialist." In internal medicine! What that really means is that he's a "fancy family doctor" and cloistered himself in a hospital a while longer in his training. By the way, young Dr. Nador is damn good. But he hasn't got what the old man has. He never could. He's got plenty, but you really can't ever go wrong with the old man. Even though he's retired. You see, Doctor, the old man has a mind like a steel trap. His son is a plugger, a hard worker, sincere, decent, and damn bright. But he'll never be the old man.

Still, he's great. But the old man is something else. He didn't have to examine me to know if I was sick. He would glance at me and know what was wrong and what should be done. He always knew what was wrong before he touched me. Very often, maybe always, he knew that my parents were wrong. I pity my parents for their naivete. They did the best they could with what they had to give. By the way, in case you haven't figured it out by now, they didn't have much to give. Like . . . nothing, or to be more accurate, almost nothing.

But the old man, Doctor, had lots to give and he wasn't stingy with love. He was and is pretty careful with money. But as I have grown to my present age, I know that being stingy with money doesn't count. "Love is not enough" is true, but love is a very great deal. To this day, the old man keeps me out of trouble. "Tell him I want to see him to give him a good lecture," he tells his son. His lectures still work. Even though his son and I both know he often is not right. When he says it, it's right enough.

The old man has always been a religious person. Not when he grew old, but he knew his God when he was a young man. He told me recently, "The Bible is the most beautiful book ever written." I smiled to express my respect for his feelings and to hide my own painful disbelief in the existence of God or gods. I wish I could believe in a God and my "immortal soul" and that death is not the end of life. But death is the end. There is no heaven, no hell, "you live while you live and then die and be done with it." And if you don't live while you can, you lose it and you never get it back. Funny, this he did teach me. "Every moment that passes," Doctor, "needs to be used fully, lovingly, creatively. There is no time to fight, to hate, to be in a bad mood. You're losing time. The watch never stops. We get only so much time."

One day I was talking with the old man and I was suddenly struck with how fast time passes. He is old, not senile, but it seems like only yesterday he was the active, busy, vigorous physician. I stupidly said, "You have become an old man." He looked at me warmly, lovingly, tears came to his eyes, and he smiled and said, "You too will someday be an old man." I was quite shaken. I realized suddenly that this old man who has meant so very much to me, at best, had like all of us but a limited number of years to live. When he dies it will be very hard for me. When one of my parents died he came to my house before anyone else got there to console and comfort me, to advise and encourage me. I wanted to see only the two Doctors Nador.

At his age, close to ninety, he is still fairly active, sees a few old patients in his study at home, and saw me and his son together recently to help me work out a problem that you and I couldn't work through. And he doesn't know what psychology is or the unconscious, or defense mechanisms. I deeply love this man and he loves me. He doesn't even know it perhaps, I mean, how he feels about me. He's going to die some day and I am very angry about that. How dare he leave me after all those years? How dare he desert and abandon me? But wait, he leaves me his son whom I will do anything for, and it has become more clear that I am slowly replacing him more and more with his son. Poor guy. Just in case he doesn't know it, son has a long way to go. I worry about the old man's death now. It could be any day, to him or anyone or you or me.

When I was a child he picked me up with his own son in bad weather and drove us to school. When I got into trouble at school he was there to stand up for me against a childish school principal. A principal who said I would not graduate from high school. I have a Ph. D., doctor, and my research is considered quite important. That is why you had to have special governmental clearance before I could see you for treatment. He took care of that school principal one-two-three. I'd like to go see that school principal and tell him all I have done. And I know perfectly well I wouldn't have done it without the love and encouragement of the little doctor. He was always behind me, telling me how good he felt I was, and I believed him a little, and it was good. He knew what my parents were like, but he never told me, and he and his wife put up with them for many years and I'm sure it was for me.

There is much about me that the little doctor would never understand which his son understands very well. There are things I've never told the old man, but he would understand. He is now too old for me to trouble him with my problems. Yet I think it might be good for him. Sometimes I'll call him to discuss something. Oh, I've really already decided what to do, but I like to stimulate the old guy. Get him thinking, perhaps arguing. It does him good. He has been more of a father to me than my own father and more of a mother than my own mother. Oh God, that I don't believe in, keep him in life for at least ten more years. No, twenty. I'm a pig. I'll settle for fifteen years. Don't let him die. I need him.

He once smiled and asked me, "How do you console an old man?" I thought fast and said, "You don't have to. You have led a good life, helped many people, often never been paid. Your life has been full. It is filled with love. From your children and grandchildren, your friends and patients and me. You will never be forgotten." Unfortunately, I don't see the little doctor much now. I am very busy, he is not. I am always afraid when the phone rings at an unusual hour. Perhaps he has gone. Please don't go. I need you. I will remember you until the day I die. I will remember you with love and tears and warmth. It's been a privilege to know you. Think of all the people that never did. He told me he loved me and cared about me since I was very young. I don't care if it's true. I believe it and that's all that counts. His son will have to take his place. You brought him up right, old Dr. Nador. He knows his responsibilities. I am one of them. He's stuck. He will inherit me from his father. Poor guy.

SECRETS IN SILLINESS

"The whole question of pledging and fraternity"

My eyes glowed with an intense excitement. I was on alert to carry out the next command that would be bellowed at me. No matter how precisely I carried out the task, I would be wrong. My words meant nothing. I was as useless as shark's dung sunk 50,000 centimeters off the southernmost tip of Sicily. I was a rat, or, to put it in more explicit terms, I was a pledge of a college fraternity.

Once a psychologist and I were having a discussion on the merits and drawbacks of fraternity life. At that time, I was a pledge of a national fraternity. Twelve weeks later, I was a brother of the fraternity. The discussion between us was a give-and-take exchange. An ex-fraternity man himself, the doctor was ranking out the myth of the college fraternity. As a pledge, I was defending as best I could the merits of fraternity and the reasons why it was necessary. However, it would not be long until I would come to see the light in regard to what fraternity and brotherhood really meant. The best defense that I could come up with was what I had been told by the brothers. I harped on the theme that it was valuable.

As I am writing this paper, there is a constant conflict in my mind as to whether or not it is right for a fraternity man to rebel against the institution which he is supposed to value with a great deal of love. But obviously, if I am able to have these thoughts, they must be somewhere in my mind. I would imagine that I would be committing political suicide if this paper ever fell into the hands of some real gung-ho fraternity man. For I am running for office. It seems I'm a hypocrite, but yet I do feel as though I could straighten out the house, even if it does not entail a deep love for the fraternity. Plus, and I may as well be rational about the whole matter, the free room is worth the aggravation of this job.

If this report is going to be judged on English grammar, or any of the more conventional ways of grading a paper, then I am completely wiped out. I'm writing this as an expose of what I presume to be my innermost feelings. The idea is to be free, and that is exactly what I intended to be. Now join me in my first pledge meeting, and continue to follow up until the present time (the writing of this paper).

The wood of the paddle had a stinging sensation as it was cracked upon my rear section. The first round consisted of six medium blows. After I gave the pledgemaster a flippant answer, I was again in "the position." Bent over, holding your "sac" with one hand, putting your other hand on your ankle, and prepared for the worst. The first meeting I had the misfortune of acting in my normal way. I was paddled fifteen times. A feeling of aggression toward the pledgemaster was building up with each belt of the paddle. I was so worked up, but yet I was helpless. I wanted to pledge, and would go through great discomfort to become a brother. Instead of striking the pledgemaster after the paddling episode, I held down my aggression. I went upstairs after the meeting had ended and let out my emotion with a good long cry. I felt as though this was the behavior of a child. Perhaps it was. When I learned that I was not the only one to have reacted in this manner, I felt better. Knowing that someone else was sharing my misery made me feel as though the crying was normal. It gave me a feeling of relief.

That same night, my "big brother" came up to talk to me about fraternity, and how everything had a purpose. The purpose of the paddling was for respect. The he went on to give me a real first-class selling job on what fraternity really was. I had thoughts of dropping out then and there, but my big brother convinced me of the merits of fraternity. I was sold. I would act with more respect and humility. I wanted fraternity, or so I thought. As the days turned into weeks, pledging became a part of me. I was residing in the fraternity house, so there was constantly the reminder that I was a pledge. The pledgemaster gave me and the rest of the pledges a beanie and a pledge pin. These were the symbols that advertised you were trying to become a member of the best fraternity on campus—so you were told. I was never without my pledge pin. I literally had it on my body 24 hours a day, 7 days a week. The threat of "God help the pledge who is caught without his pledge pin" kept ringing in my mind. The saying brought the pin in the shower and into the bed.

I tried to be what was considered a good pledge, while not having to rely on brown-nosing and being a yes man. It was hard for me to assume the yes man role. I was the type of person who was not afraid to speak out for or against something I believed in. Pledging put a restriction on my aggressive tendencies. Fortunately, I had control of them most of the time. A worker in my pledge class, I often stayed up late into the night doing some sort of task for the fraternity. However, I was wise enough to know my own capabilities, and if at any time schoolwork was a pressing issue, I would simply tell the brothers that I had to study. They either liked it or lumped it. I kept on telling the brothers that I would be of no value to them if I were not in school. Most of the time the brothers showed wise judgment and gave me permission to study. If they did not, I would tell them where to go, brother or no brother. Naturally, I would have to make a formal apology to the brother and ask forgiveness for my misbehavior. Oh, how humble can one get!

I was pleased to find out that during social functions a pledge was on the same equal basis as a brother. This was really an accomplishment. Imagine, to be able to talk to a brother in a natural manner. No longer was there the invisible wall that separated the brother from the pledge. I could act myself. Well, at least as close to myself as I thought wise. There was always the thought in my mind that any actions which I might display that did not seem proper for a pledge would be brought up at the next pledge meeting. Therefore, I had to act in a fairly disciplined manner. Never did I let myself fully unwind.

Everything has a purpose. Everything has a purpose. Everything has a purpose. Over and over, this statement was hammered into my head. If a brother told me to count the windows in the Y.M.C.A., I was supposed to believe that this would bring me closer to the meaning of fraternity. They told me that many of my pledge tasks would seem as though they didn't have a purpose, but that they really did, believe it or not. If you were disrespectful enough to ask the purpose, you knew that you were asking for trouble. I could not accept some of the beating-around-the-bush answers to questions.

The weeks rolled by. The numbers of the pledge class were rapidly diminishing. Most of the pledges who dropped either could not take the mental and physical hazing, or they were having trouble in school. The fraternity dropped a few more, for they were not the proper image of the type of person who should represent their fraternity—if it means anything. All told, thirteen pledges left the ranks. Finally, I received the letter from the fraternity informing me that the brotherhood had taken a vote and I had been ACCEPTED. This should have been one of the happiest days in my life. But somehow I was more relieved than happy. My happiness was of a subdued nature. After twelve weeks of a memorable ordeal, the fraternity accepted me. I belonged!

I now became disillusioned. Had I done the right thing in pledging in the first place? Was this really what I wanted? Sure, I had made many close friends, but friends had always been easy for me to make. Perhaps the entire episode was a waste of time and energy. There were times of enjoyment, but I could also have enjoyed myself without the fraternity. Did I join because I was not secure in my own thinking of what I really wanted out of life? All of these questions wandered around in my mind. I would answer these questions in time, as long as I kept an open mind and thought for myself.

The initiation program was to me unimpressive. I was never one for ceremonies and secret vows, and this was no exception. I witnessed (when not blindfolded) the entire solemn affair with a grain of salt. After the initiation to brotherhood ceremony was over, the secret meeting that I had always envisioned was about to get under way. The brothers surrounding me told me the first meeting would really impress me. It did not.

I went to bed that night wondering if I had not made a mistake by pledging. The pledge policy I thought was foolish. Now that I was a brother and had therefore attained my goal, I was disappointed. The invisible wall was no longer present. People acted like people did everywhere. The brotherhood I had wanted so much had its faults, just like any other group of people.

Cliques that I was unaware of as a pledge came to the surface in a short time. Some brothers did not even associate with other brothers. But still, the fraternity went along, living in its made-up utopia.

Perhaps the greatest shock that I received in the fraternity meeting was when some of my pledge brothers were brought up for brotherhood. To me it was the most fruitless scene I had witnessed in a long time. Brothers who had nothing to say held the floor for long, boring periods of time, rambling on about how a particular pledge was unworthy of HIS fraternity. These brothers knew the pledge only as a pledge, not as the real person on an equal basis when you feel that he is below you. The brothers have this superiority feeling. I suppose that everyone likes to feel superior. But the way they picked apart the individual, limb from limb, was really upsetting. I couldn't believe what I was hearing. I imagined how the discussion went when I was brought up for brotherhood. After a 3 hr. marathon on a pledge who had pledged fourteen weeks, the final vote ended up with a blackball. My stomach turned with disgust.

These were now my fraternity brothers and my fraternity, yet I felt as though I wanted no part of it. But I had obligated myself to the fraternity both monetarily and socially. Many of my closest friends were in my pledge class. I would now have to act like the other brothers in trying to establish the fact that certain pledges were ready for brotherhood. I now started to question the idea of whether there was any difference between a close friend and a brother. I concluded that the only distinction between the two was that the brother had a fraternity oath that was supposed to bind him to all other brothers. Once again I wondered.

Why are some people so interested in fraternity? Each year the new pledge class is larger. I assume that the prospective pledges have heard stories of what it means to be a pledge, yet they still come in droves, anxiously waiting to be made complete asses of. There certainly must be a strong inner drive in each pledge which helps him absorb all the guff that is handed out. Perhaps they think, as did I, that the fraternity is some sort of utopia, where things are just too good to be true. Everything he has ever dreamed or heard of, and things that he wanted to be a part of—girls, booze, parties, friends—would be at his fingertips. He must hope to be a silver spoke in the great golden wheel.

I notice in the present pledge class the inner struggle of the individual to wants to belong to my secret fraternity. These pledges do not know what is behind the wall (perhaps if they did, they would not pledge), yet they will put up with all types of ridiculous tasks and hazing. Once they are on the other side of the wall, a few, like myself, may give time to ponder the whole question of pledging and fraternity itself.

There comes a time in the life of a pledge when he goes through a series of asinine ordeals, devised by the most frustrated brothers, and in a capsule it is called hell night, or week, depending upon the amount of sadism in the group. The period of ordeal is supposed to make or break the pledge. I do not take part in these "horror shows." The older brothers told me it would make the pledge have more respect for the fraternity, while he was pledging. If anything, it has the opposite result. The purpose behind hell week, in my view, is to allow the frustrations of certain brothers to be taken out on the innocent pledge. It reminded me of the behavior of uncivilized, let alone unsophisticated, children, not grown men in college.

To the pledges of the new class, I have an attitude that most of the brothers do not reflect. I believe that if the individual wants the fraternity and meets some of its qualifications (obviously I have become a little particular without even realizing it), then let the person in.

So, we have seen my progress and reactions from pledge to brother, to the writing of this paper. What will likely happen is that I will play the fraternity game for a year or two, and then I may have enough courage to admit to myself that I was kidding myself. The possibilities that my attitude toward the ideals of fraternity, as I understand them today, might change seem slight. The experience which I gained in this adventure has helped me to have a better insight into the thoughts and behavior of other people. This in itself is priceless knowledge.

WHEN THREE
EQUALS NINE

"The impact of an accidental pregnancy"

When my wife and I married, we had just turned nineteen. At the time of our marriage, she was six months pregnant. She was working and living at home with her parents. I had just finished the first term of my sophomore year at college and was living at home. Up until two weeks before we were married, no one knew that she was pregnant. Everyone in our home town thought we were the couple that never engaged in any sexual activity other than maybe necking. There were many people who were quite surprised when word traveled along the grapevine of the town.

Because of what I had always heard from my parents, teachers, and priests concerning sex and teenagers, and because of the position I was in, I had many experiences, before and since my marriage, that created a great deal of tension and anxiety for me. These occurred in everyday interactions.

I didn't know how to tell people that I was getting married and my wife was pregnant. Would they think that it could have happened to them? Would they think it was normal sex behavior for a young couple to have intercourse, and because they didn't realize fully what they were doing and the consequences of their actions, that the girl might get pregnant? Would they react as if there were something unusual about the whole thing? Would they think that I was something dirty and all I had ever done was take a girl into the woods to see how much I could get? Would my friends make fun of me because I "knocked up" a girl? If I was walking down the street toward another person, would he cross the street to avoid me because I was a dirty person? There were so many things I would ask myself. Maybe some would turn out to be true and maybe some were foolish, but I still couldn't help but ask myself these questions many times.

There were two people whom I wanted to tell that I was getting married before someone else told them. They were my principal and science teacher in high school. I had known them for some time and had always been able to go to either one for advice when I needed it. I knew they would be surprised, since I had just started school. I thought they might be a little disappointed at the thought of my wife being pregnant at the time of my marriage, but I was quite sure they wouldn't call me a bum and tell me not to bother them.

They reacted pretty much as I had expected them to. They knew it was too late for lectures on what not to do and they both wanted to help me. Both of them told me to come to them if I needed money for tuition or to buy the baby a pair of shoes.

They pointed out to me that I would find out who my real friends were. These would be the people who would have the same feelings toward me as they always had. On the other hand, there would be people who would change their attitudes toward me. I now think that people who react this way in this situation are very foolish and ignorant. I found that there are people who changed their attitudes toward me and there are those who haven't, such as these two high school people. I consider them to be very good friends, for they gave me moral support when I most needed it and they would do so again if it every became necessary.

So far I haven't found anyone who has changed his attitude toward me directly because of my getting married and already having my wife pregnant. I am still friendly with everyone, but we don't have the same interests or the same things in common.

I think this is because I have someone else to spend my time with and don't have the time to do any of the things that a single man does. Many of my friends still like to go drinking five miles from nowhere and get stinking drunk. My attitude toward this, since I have been married, is a little different from theirs. But I don't worry too much about the relationship I have with them.

I was married on a Wednesday night and had to return to school the next day. I didn't want anybody at school to know that I was married. I would take my wedding ring off before I got to school and put it in my pocket, and when I got out of school I would put it back on. This was a ridiculous and very immature thing to do, but nevertheless I did it.

A good question to ask myself now is, "Why didn't I want anyone to know that I was married?" Was it because everyone thinks that nineteen is too young for a person to get married, especially in the middle of his second year of college? The only reason a person in this position would get married is if he got his girl friend pregnant. Maybe I didn't want them to know that this was why I was getting married now, while in such an insecure position, instead of waiting four or five years.

Nobody at school knew that I was getting married and I was afraid of the questions that they would ask. I didn't know how I would answer them. Should I come right out and tell them why? Or should I tell them it is none of their business? Or that I got married for the same reasons as everybody else?

Another question that I can ask is, "Why was I afraid to say that my wife was already pregnant and we were just married?"

Society says that a couple is not supposed to engage in intercourse until they are married. The church says the same thing. I had heard this all my life. That it was the wrong thing to do as well as an evil and sinful act. Because I had always heard that it was sinful and evil to do these things, and even a worse thing to be found out or exposed by a premarital pregnancy. I considered myself an evil person and didn't want to be thought of as such a person by my peers and professors.

After two weeks of not wearing my ring at school, I finally began to wear it. One day before class I met several students I knew well. One of the boys said he heard that I had just gotten married. I broke out in a sweat and my legs felt a little weak. This was the first time that anyone had mentioned it to me. I was almost afraid of them and I wanted to run away before they could say anything else. I said that I had been married for a couple of weeks and showed them the wedding ring, which was on the hand I had just taken from my pocket. They didn't ask any more questions in regard to this, but I felt as if they were trying to figure out why I had gotten married all of a sudden and had never mentioned it.

I was quite relieved when they left. I walked into the classroom with another boy who also asked me if I was married. I didn't know him any better than I did anybody else in school and he didn't know me very well. But I told him that I was married and my wife was already pregnant. It didn't even bother me to tell him. Why, I don't know. Could it have been that I felt guilty about being married and no one knowing about it and I wanted to tell someone? Maybe I wanted him to know so he could tell the rest and I wouldn't worry about them not knowing that my wife was pregnant. If they knew, maybe they wouldn't put me in an awkward position by asking me questions.

Why should I worry about whether or not the other boys know that my wife is pregnant? Many of them could get a girl pregnant or have intercourse with many girls but are just not as unfortunate.

One day I was sitting in a classroom with three of the boys who didn't know I was married. They were talking about all their troubles and how much they had to worry about. I thought to myself that they think they have a lot of troubles, so I told them that I was married. They all looked at me with surprised faces. One of them asked if my wife worked and I said no, that she was pregnant and couldn't work. Word soon got around that I was married and my wife was expecting and I was relieved that everyone now knew what I didn't want to have to tell them. When my son was born I was very happy and proud as any new father is. I still felt funny when talking to someone and telling them I was married and had a child. I was afraid they would ask how long I had been married and what they would think when I told them three months.

I didn't come to school the day my son was born and I couldn't help but wonder how the boys at school would react the next day. I didn't see why they should react any differently to me than to anyone else who had just become a father, but I still thought about it.

The next day I went back to school and for the next couple of days just about everyone congratulated me. It didn't make any difference to them how long I had been married, at least it seemed that way.

I couldn't wait to tell my friends at home. It didn't bother me to talk to these people. They had always reacted toward me after I was married the same as before.

For the next several months I was always nervous if I told someone that I was married and a father. Most people would ask how long I had been married and how old my child was. I felt that they would be counting months to see if everything added up. I don't imagine everyone that I talked to added up the months because they probably didn't care, but I still felt awfully uncomfortable with some people.

Now that I have been married for several years and my child is growing up, I don't feel the same tension as I did.

I recently went for an interview for a job. During the interview the employer asked my how long I had been married, so I told him. He then asked how old my child was and I answered him without hesitation. Then I thought to myself, maybe he's doing a little arithmetic, and if he is, and he doesn't like it, I know what he can do with it. I didn't get the job but I know, or hope, that his arithmetic, if he did any, had no bearing on his decision.

As I have just said, my attitude concerning what other people think of me with regard to my marriage has changed. I think that this change can be attributed to several things.

I first decided that it was none of anyone's business but mine. I'm the one that got married and I'm the one who has to support my family, and I'm the one who still has to go to school, and I'm the one who has to worry about these things.

If a teenage couple get married and the girl is pregnant, all anybody can do is accept it. When I say anybody, I mean parents, clergymen, and anybody who knows the couple. It may be a little hard for some people to accept if they want to think that things like this don't happen, and if they do happen, it is to someone they don't know.

When I went to my priest to tell him I wanted to get married, he asked me why I had waited for six months to reach this decision. All I said was that I was afraid. I didn't really know what I was afraid of, but I was afraid. He told me I was afraid of reality and that I had to face up to it.

I think this is why you have to accept something such as this.

Once it happens, you have to face up to it. It is real and you can't say, "Hold it, I made a mistake so I'll erase it and start over again."

NOT THE SABBATH

"Hostility, and other reactions to death"

My grandmother lived with us during my adolescence. Since she was a very devout Jew, it became necessary for everyone in the household to follow suit so far as our religion was concerned. I therefore became a patriot of Judaism. I proceeded to the synagogue every Friday evening to welcome the Sabbath as well as every Saturday morning, to participate in the conduct of the services. This routine went on for three years, until I was twelve years old. It was at this time that my mother became very ill and was forced to be hospitalized. Being the youngest in the family, I naturally was not told about her sickness, but I would visit my mother at least twice a week. On these visits there was no formal conversation carried on. There was a big plastic tent around her bed and all one was able to do was to wave, hopefully getting a return wave, and when I attended, maybe even a smile. My visitations lasted no longer than ten to fifteen minutes, when I would be immediately whisked out of the room and be told to wait until the others had returned.

As the days went on, I could tell that something was wrong. People were visiting the house and crying. My aunts and uncles started to gather around the house, approaching me for ab-solutely no reason, patting me on the head, and telling me not to worry, that everything would be all right . . . everything will be fine. It was then that my grandmother came up to me and told me to go to the synagogue and attend the Sabbath services.

It was on that Saturday, the day before Mother's Day, that I began to proceed to the synagogue to fulfill my obligation to my grandmother and to pray for Mom and attend the Sabbath services. I used to enjoy attending Saturday services because of a particular man who has long since passed away. His name was Mr. Mayer. He was an elderly man of maybe seventy or seventy-five years of age, but a very smart man. He somehow made me feel comfortable and at ease, whereas I had always felt out of place with the other men, who always kept to themselves and had nothing to do with me. He would always surprise me if I had done my lesson well for that day. He knew of the trouble in my household, and told me that he also was praying for my mther. When I told him about the plight in my home and of how everyone seemed concerned, he said, "Don't worry. God never takes anyone away on the Sabbath." I believed him, for as I said before, he was a very wise man.

After the services, I received my candy from Mr. Mayer and ran home. I stayed in front of the house that afternoon and was just fooling around and playing, mostly cowboy games, with the other kids, when I suddenly heard my grandmother calling for me. I ran up the stairs and saw everybody in the corridor crying. It was a terrible and very uncomfortable atmosphere. My father and grandmother then told me to come out to the back porch. While walking down the hall, my grandmother started to cry and she fell to the floor, at which time everybody ran over to her. My father continued walking with me to the porch and told me in a somewhat broken up fashion that Ma had died.

It somehow did not ring a bell. I did not know what to do, nor how to react, as I had never experienced anything like this before. I did not know what was expected of me, nor what to expect. By this time, my father was on his knees in front of me, crying like a baby. Still not knowing what to do, I turned around, ignoring all the people still lined up in the hall, and went to my room and closed the door. The noise and crying were still going on outside and the only thing that I could remember was what Mr. Mayer had said—God never takes anyone away on a Sabbath.

My mother was only forty years old when she died. She was a good person and we had a lot of fun together. We never had a car, but somehow we managed always to go out on a Sunday afternoon ride with my aunt and her family. These thoughts and many others of this type were going through my mind like flashes as I sat in my room looking out the window. During that whole time while my mother was in the hospital, it was not as if I would never see her again, for everyone told me that she was fine and would soon be home with us. My weekly visits, although only fifteen minutes in length, gave increased thoughts in my mind that she would surely be home, for I did not know at that time that a blood clot was speeding to her brain.

As time went by, people came into my room crying, rubbing their hands through my hair, messing it all up, and telling me not to worry. My aunts began covering all the mirrors in the house with towels and tablecloths, and in the living room a huge candle was lit. A Rabbi came into the room and told me that I would have to go to the synagogue every morning and every evening of every week for an entire year and say Kaddish. This is a mourner's prayer that the male children in a Jewish family say for the deceased parent, out of respect. I did not want to go because had it not been for my grandmother, I really wouldn't have wanted to go on Saturdays either, even less so now, because it was as though God had lied; for, in spite of what Mr. Mayer had said, He did take her away on the Sabbath. It was at this time during my life that I first started to ask the question "why." To this very day I still ask the question "why." You might call me an atheist if you wish.

I then was told to get dressed, as I would have to go to the funeral parlor that evening. In the Jewish religion, as soon as a death occurs, prayers are said, and the person is buried within a period of two days. After I had gotten dressed, time seemed to go by very slowly before we finally left for the funeral parlor. I had never been to a funeral parlor before. I had never seen a dead person before. It is true that we used to play games after seeing people in the movies getting killed, but it was somehow unreal now. In the movies, even at this age, we know that the star has not actually been killed and that even though he plays dead, he will be alive in real life. I could not visualize a real dead body. I can remember at that time trying to think about it, but at the same time trying not to, because it gave me the creeps.

My thoughts were quickly taken from me as it was finally time to leave. The consoling and mourning and the hands through my hair occurred over and over. Now it was beginning to be annoying. "Why don't they leave me alone, why don't they go home where they belong. I never see them anyway." People kept saying over and over again, "She was so young. She had everything to live for. She did not even see her son get Bar-Mitzvah." Every time they would mention the word Bar-Mitzvah, which is comparable to a confirmation, the screaming would get worse and the people would run to me, shaking their heads and crying all the more.

We finally arrived at the funeral parlor. It was a small brick building with a huge awning that ran from the stairway all the way out to the street. When we entered, a host of men all attired in black approached us and told us how sorry they were and not to worry because everything had been taken care of. These were the undertakers. These men immediately flew off into different directions, telling all the people congregated in the hallway to take their seats, for the mourning party had arrived. At the same time, another man, all dressed in black, told us to follow him. My brother, who is older than I, was crying hysterically while holding onto my hand; my father was standing behind me. We walked into a large room which had wooden benches on each side, as one sees in a church or synagogue. At the extreme end of the room was a platform with a huge coffin on top of it. To the right of the coffin was an elderly man with a long white beard, who kept rocking back and forth chanting prayers in a low monotone. We finally got to the front row and saw down. This same undertaker who led us down the aisle began to pin black ribbons on the clothing of each of the mourning party. The Rabbi then came forward and with scissors cut the ribbon, while at the same time still chanting prayers. He then told us to go up and see my mother.

It did not look like her. She was so still and quiet and white. My hands were holding the side of the coffin, and it was only natural for me to reach out and touch her hand. I will never forget this as long as I live, for it was not the hand that I had known and that was so familiar to me. It was cold and clammy and unreal. The man in black told me not to touch her. In the meantime, my father and sister were still crying and, as if in unison, as soon as they began to cry, the other people in the room would cry, too.

I could not watch this any longer. I don't know why, but I went back to the bench and began to cry more hysterically than anyone in the entire room. I could not control myself: I could not stop. Worst of all, I did not know what I was crying about. The only thing that I was sure about was that God had lied. Mr. Mayer had lied. I felt that there was no point in going to the synagogue and praying and that there was no point for this Jewish ceremony that we were having now. For the rest of that night, during the service, as well as during the service the following morning when she was buried, I never approached the coffin again to see my mother. I was asked to and I wanted to, for I loved her very much, but the mother that I had loved and the unreal thing that I saw in that coffin were not one and the same, and I could only wish that this experience would end as soon as possible.

For one year I went to the synagogue out of respect to my mother. As I said previously, there were two services daily. I attended both of them, one at 6:30 every morning and the other at 7:30 every evening, including Saturdays and Sundays. I did not want to go, nor did I believe in what I was doing and what I was saying, but because of respect and because everyone said that it was a wonderful thing that I was doing, I continued to attend faithfully.

Since that day, I have seen several people pass on. It was only a few months ago that a very close friend of mine was taken away at the age of 26, leaving a wife and child. When I attended his funeral, the Rabbi said during his eulogy that God had wanted him, that He had a purpose in mind for him, and that he was going away to a world far better than the present world in which we live. As soon as I heard this, I could only think of one thing. How foolish a man this Rabbi is! How foolish is anybody in this parlor who believes in what this man is preaching, for how can anybody console others by telling them to believe in something that he knows not from fact but merely from blind faith. How can anybody as good as he at twenty-six years of age, or as good as my mother at forty years of age, be taken away with the excuse that someone by the name of God wanted them more than we here on earth do?

Sure, there must be a God—there must be a Supreme Being,

but who are we, if there is a Supreme Being? Who are we as mere mortals to attach immortality to any Supreme Being and actually believe that there is a true so-called Garden of Eden in the hereafter that we will eventually end up in. It is my belief that all religions, whether they be Christianity, Judaism, or what have you, are all a bunch of wishful thinkers. If there is a true God, whatever His title may be, how can He possibly stand by and watch six million people put to death in the most brutal manner which man can possibly devise? How can He possibly stand by idly and allow world war after world war to go on generation after generation, men killing men? How can this be true? Why is it that all miracles and everything else on this mumbo-jumbo line that we study in the Old Testament and the New Testament start and stop in the Bible.

During that period of my adolescence until the present day, I have constantly asked the question "why." To this day I am thoroughly convinced that there can only be one answer. Religion is a way in which a weak person can face the grim realities of life and death. Religion is a method in which man can find an escape to something that he knows nothing of, but fears. Religion is a means by which man can cope with fear through blind faith. I myself am afraid of death. I do not know of anyone who has returned from death to report on what death is. Death to me is distinguished by sorrow, and through my experience it is not something to be looked forward to. I do not know what death will bring me. I do know this: that in my present situation I do like life very much. Death to me takes me away from the life that I like and that I know. Death to me brings a fear of unknowingness which I panic thinking about. I cannot forsee any Almighty Being taking me away to live with him in a dreamed-up world of which I know nothing.

This event of my mother's death, along with the deaths of many people who were taken away from me and from this present world, has made me become a man without a faith in religion, and although this feeling does not coincide with modern thinking, I do not feel badly about it.

LITTLE PLASTER MAN

"Attaining relative maturity"

I was born in Canada at which time my father was in Japan. My first year of life was spent with three women. These were my mother, older sister, and grandmother. Naturally, I was babied because all three waited on me hand and foot. According to child psychology, the first year is very important in determining how the child will see the world. I saw the world through a "milk bottle." My every need was fulfilled and I began to see the world as a nice place with nice people. At this time the war was still on, so most of the men were gone, leaving only women around the neighborhood. This meant even when taken out for a walk I came in contact with women. I heard, saw, and smelled nothing but women for the first year of my life. This sort of environment made me self-centered and all I had to do was cry and my wish was fulfilled. However, this abruptly changed when father returned from the service. He found me a spoiled brat and decided it was time to start making a man out of me. I remember when he first picked me up, I screamed bloody murder. I was scared to death, because he was the first man to touch me. The louder I screamed, the more he laughed and the more frightened I became. I began to hate all men and wanted only women to touch me. This was a natural outcome of being raised and pampered by women, and it was a long time before this fear subsided.

Two years later we moved to another town where I was to spend the next four years overcoming the fear of father. He was a carpenter and worked in a shop not far from home. Our home was a small bungalow located in a quiet part of town. The house had a small lawn in front with a little plaster man standing in the middle holding a fishing pole. At first glance the pole resembled a penis and we named the statue "Little Willie," The name scared me and for some reason I gave this name to my penis. I could never decide if I liked the statue or not. One day I would and the next day I'd be scared to death to look at it. Possibly I saw father standing there with a large penis.

This can be related to being brought up by women. I am assuming they didn't let me touch my genital organs because they thought it wrong and therefore I thought touching or looking at Little Willie was wrong. My fear of this object was very intense, as was my fear of father. This fear kept building up and when I was four years old I had a terrible experience concerning Little Willie.

One day I awoke to find Willie trampled by a cow. I was scared stiff and cried all day. I remember I didn't cry because Willie was gone but because he was broken into pieces. I felt this pain in my genital area and possibly I thought I would lose my genitals now that Willie was gone. It took me a long time to forget this and I was never sure if a cow or father had broken him. I was always suspicious of father and this helped manifest my fear of him.

I thought of father as someone who was out to get me. He was a large man with a lot of strength and courage. He was covered with hair and always dirty and sweaty from work. I didn't like him because he was dirty and I was clean and neat. He used to pick me up and rub his unshaven face against mine; this not only hurt but enhanced my fear of him. I was close to mother because I was used to women. I hated father because he was receiving more love from mother. I saw him as someone who wanted to destroy me and have mother all for himself. I have often thought about this part of my childhood, but I could never explain it.

It was a long time before I saw father as a nurturant person in my life. It took only one episode for me to view father as someone who wanted and loved me.

One day I broke into a chicken pen and started beating the chickens with a stick. While my back was turned a rooster started biting the back of my knees. I had on short pants and the rooster was making a mess of my leg. I screamed for help and luckily enough father heard me. He rescued me from the rooster and at this point I saw him as a totally different person. He looked at my leg, patched it up, and sent me home. I realized from this experience that father was someone who loved and wanted me and could offer me protection. Now I wanted to be like father. I wanted to be like him not only to acquire the same amount of love from mother he received, but I wanted to be brave and strong. I wanted to get dirty and sweaty and wear old clothes.

At this point, I would like to pick up a loose end concerning the chicken pen episode. Why was I beating the chickens in the first place? I believe this can best be explained by referring to the cow that trampled Willie. I became scared of cows and I started to despise them. Because a cow is an animal, I began to hate all animals. I saw them as poor creatures without brains. I could not take my hatred out on cows because they were too large, but chickens were small enough so they couldn't retaliate. I wanted to hurt the chickens the same way the cow had hurt me. I also mistreated our cat. One day I poured kerosene on his back and his back bent so much his stomach dragged on the ground. It gave me pleasure to see the cat squirm and twist in pain. As I think about it now, this might have had sexual connotation. Possibly I was a sadist and received sexual gratification by inflicting and witnessing pain. This explanation is, of course, only a thought and I believe a better explanation can be found in the relations with my parents. They were strict with me and possibly I wanted to treat animals the way I was treated. I resented the authority of my parents and decided I wanted authority also. Because I was too small to tell adults what to do, I believe I started to show animals I had some authority over them. This allowed me to release my aggression upon animals instead of people.

During the last two years in Canada there were no significant experiences that influenced my life. It was a small town and life there was not too demanding. There were no girls in my neighborhood, so I didn't have a chance to find out there was a difference between the sexes. I summarized there must be a difference because one day we went visiting some friends who had a girl. After playing for a while, she took off her pants but kept her skirt on. We continued to play for a while and then her mother came out. When she saw the pants on the ground she made us stop playing together. This experience haunted my mind for a while and I was interested to find out what she had that I hadn't. I didn't want to ask father and after a short time I forgot about the whole affair.

I began to center my life around what father was doing. I liked to go places and do things with him. I wanted to act and think like him, and at the same time I didn't obey mother as much as father. I wanted him to tell me what I could and couldn't do.

I saw him as the perfect man and I wanted to be just like him. He was now planning to go to America and work there. I was now eight years old and the trip to the United States was a thrilling experience for me.

The drive to America was a great experience, but I didn't like the idea of leaving all my relatives. It gave me an insecure feeling because I was leaving part of my family behind. I feel this experience helped strengthen my identification with father. He was the only man I knew in this country, so I looked to him for security and protection. We had a close family in comparison with American families. My parents were raised under old country discipline and so was I. Our new neighbors thought I was a perfect gentleman, the way I spoke and acted, but my new friends thought I was a sissy because I always obeyed my parents. This caused a great deal of anxiety because I wanted to be one of them and, at the same time, my parents demanded that I follow their strict commands.

My social status among peers became very low, even though I had a good identification with father. The reason for this can be attributed to the fact that father had different values than my peers. His values consisted of honesty, respect, courage, and hard work. He realized I was having trouble with my peers, so one day he told me, "If anyone calls you a chicken and you don't fight to disprove it, don't bother to come home again." This really shook me up, but it was all I needed to give me courage to stand up to my peers.

The following day I had a fight with one of the group's leaders. Although I was scared to death, I won the fight and eventually the respect of my peers. They accepted me into the group and this made me feel like someone. I began to see myself as a capable individual with confidence in myself and what I did. This helped me do better in school subjects and sports. I began to enjoy sports very much. As with every boy, my life centered around football. I loved the game, but my father never played with me. He thought I was wasting my time. He never changed his views on sports and I feel this had a great influence on me in later life.

Up until the ninth grade, father and I were very close. We used to work together building things and remodeling the house. I used to help him with his job and and we got along fine, until I asked him to go fishing or play ball. He kept telling me sports were a waste of time and I should spend more time working around the house. My favorite sport was football and my sophomore year I made the first string. This was a great achievement for me and I was very happy about it. All my friends and neighbors cheered me on, but I felt very lonely because father hardly ever went to watch me play. I became more withdrawn from him and at times it seemed I didn't know him. I felt lost and alone because the other boys' fathers were always at the games to watch them play. I started to become withdrawn from my friends because I was jealous of them.

My withdrawal from Father and friends dealt a tremendous blow to my personality. In the lower grades I had a lot of fun and enjoyed being with people. I was group-oriented. Everything the group did, I did with them. I was a leader and enjoyed the responsibility of making plans for parties and such. I was looked up to by my classmates for being a good athlete and student. All this changed when I started to withdraw from my friends. I was still considered a leader and during my junior and senior years in high school I was president of the class. This didn't change my personality, knowing people still looked up to me. I didn't act conceited or anything, but instead I became quiet and passive. I began to think for myself more and more. I didn't rely on anyone, not even father, to help me with my problems. I went off by myself and thought about things and analyzed my problems by myself. I began to show resentment toward father for his lack of interest in school activities.

I showed this resentment by doing the opposite of what he told me to do. He wanted me to work, so I decided to loaf. He wanted me to join the service, so I decided to go to college. Everything he planned for me I did just the opposite. I hoped it would make him feel hurt if I thought for myself and in this way I could get back at him for hurting me. Although my personality changed greatly toward him, it didn't change too much toward my peers. I would like to give my explanation of a factor I think greatly influences a person's personality.

I feel a child's personality depends greatly on his parents' personalities. If his parents are quiet and passive, I believe the child will see these factors as something he should have. Using my parents as an example, I would like to see if their personalities are the same as mine.

Both parents are very quiet, passive, and easygoing. I feel this is attributed to their being foreigners. They never made any really close friends (friends they visited and went places with) in America. They kept to themselves and they wanted me to do the same. I feel they became jealous of my having so many friends. Possibly they thought they would lose me if they allowed me too much freedom and friends. I wanted to show them I still loved them, so I developed my personality like theirs in order to make them feel I wanted to be like them. This was a tremendous pressure on me and one day it was all released when I found out my mother was pregnant. I realized this would give me a chance to live my own life, because I knew they would have to spend much of their time with the new baby. This was what actually happened and I began to feel like a new person. Father stopped telling me what to do and I began to think more for myself. I was so happy gaining my freedom that I started to help around the house. I wanted to help because it was my own idea. No one told me what to do and this gave me a feeling of complete independence. I started to make my own dentist ʎond doctor appointments and at first this really scared me. I could feel myself becoming very independent, but at the same time I felt insecure.

I believe this was the turning point of my life. Although it was a slow and painful transition, I went from complete dependence to complete independence. As I look back now, I believe this was the way father planned it. When I decided to enter college instead of the service, father didn't say anything about it. I knew he wanted me to go in the army and become a man, but when I asked him what he thought about my going to college, he said it was up to me. He said I'd have to make the decision myself, that he couldn't help me. Well, as you can see, I decided to go to college and I'm glad I did. I enjoy college very much and I'm working part time in order to put myself through. It's a great experience to realize you're on your own, and I can honestly say I wouldn't want it any other way. I am completely on my own and thinking for myself. I'm not easily influenced by other people and although I'm still not sure what I really want out of life, I feel I am quite capable of making the right decisions in order to reach the goals I have now set for myself.

In conclusion, as I look back on my life and see the things that influenced my present thinking and actions, I can see how easily I could have become a totally different person. If just one small episode had been changed, my whole personality might have turned out completely different from what it is now.

The experiences I have written about have been bothering me for a long time, but I never believed they could influence and shape my life the way they have. I thought these experiences were unique and could never happen to anyone else, but I realize now they are common to everyone in one way or another. I have realized I'm a normal person facing the same conflicts as everyone else traveling the long road to adulthood.

WALLS COME TUMBLING

"Shattering of a 'nice, meaningful world'"

I have learned from historians that there are many religions and all of them claim to be right yet have done wrong; that there were many wars and much politics but little concern for right and wrong; that the story of history is one sentence long: Man is born, he suffers, he dies!

I have learned from political scientists that good old democracy is not accepted as right all over; that, in fact, it has an ideological enemy called communism. I have learned from Marx that capitalists are exploiting me and religion is an opiate for the masses.

I have learned from anthropoligists that man lives in a civilized jungle where survival of the fittest still rules; that man is a sub-order of primates known as homosapiens; that among his cousins are Limers, Tasiers, monkeys, and apes; that my ancestors were Australopithecinae or man-apes from South Africa; that, in short, man is an animal who doesn't like to admit it. I have learned from anthropoligists that there are many societies.

I have learned from astronomers and geologists that the earth is an insignificant hunk of metal and rock, in one of a billion insignificant solar systems; that it whirls around in space at a phenomenal speed for a phenomenal distance; and that it is precariously balanced by conflicting forces of gravity—a magical substance we cannot see.

I have learned from psychologists that I am not a truly rational being; that I am a spiritual battlefield between the "id," the "ego," and the "superego;" that I pass through various stages of development, as a product passes through a conveyor belt in a factory; that I was born a savage baby—a bundle of drives and that cultures and environment have so wonderfully civilized me, as they civilized Hitler, Mussolini, Stalin, Chou

En Lei, Machiavelli, and Marx.

I have been told that I long to die and return to the womb; that outwardly I'm an adult but inwardly I'm still a child; that I project, that I rationalize, and that I repress; yes, particularly that I repress. I have been told that whether I'm distrustful, shameful, doubtful, or feel guilty; that whether I'm impulsive, aggressive, or introverted, withdrawn, or meek, is dependent on the way I was weaned and toilet trained. I have learned that I'm motivated by a pleasure principle and that I'm sexually frustrated but don't know it, or at least don't dare to realize it. Finally, that I'm in a period termed adolescence or young adulthood, or, as Freud called it, the genital stage; that outside of gaining pleasure derived from mature sexual relations with the opposite sex—which I'm not allowed to have—I am primarily concerned with those silly questions: What is it all about? Who am I? Where am I going and why? In short, I have learned that I am nothing better than a modified "id," and a confused one at that!

Let me relate to you my experience since entering college. I am a psychology major and I plan on doing social work, whatever that might be. When I think back, I was guided toward this direction by my religion and the contact I had with an emotionally disturbed friend. I was a good Catholic, if there is such a thing, and I came to school to carry out the mission God had sent me on. The point is, I came to school with ideals and my life had meaning. I felt secure in my society, in my family, in my religion, with my God. I was confident that the world was all right. It was all right because it had meaning, because it was humane, because it was divinely created.

It took 12 years for me to obtain that all-important high school diploma, which seems so insignificant now. During this process I was taught, although some say indoctrinated, that democracy was good and communism was bad; that this country was right, morally and socially, and that *that* country was wrong. I felt that patriotism, loyalty, and faith in God were genuine, good, and widespread. I knew my religion was right and that *theirs* was misguided. The Bible was infallible and Christianity was the answer to the problems of the world. I thought this was general knowledge and all intelligent people knew it.

Yes, I came to college, and lo and behold, my nice meaningful world was shattered—for this I was bitter, frustrated, and depressed. For the first time I felt that terrible void. And the questions came flowing out. What am I doing here? Where am I going? Why? What does it all mean? It seemed ironic that I was paying to become confused and frustrated.

In relating this to myself, and in view of the fact that my old world is irretrievably lost, I, as many college students, am trying to adjust and find a new perspective in my life. During the past two years, knowing where I'm going and why or, in short, what is the meaning of my life, has been most important.

I realize I'm going through a normal stage and that I will adjust to it. The thing that concerns me is how I will adjust. A person could find meaning in his life by his achievement or accomplishment. But is accomplishment enough motivation in itself? If a person, for example, drilled little holes in little parts that go into other parts and other parts and other parts that make up a final part or product, and never know the purpose of his work except to make money, he cannot, in my opinion, find meaning in his work. This person must find meaning elsewhere, someone he loves, a religion, some other goal, possibly even suffering.

I might find some meaning in my life by the career I pursue. Of course, this depends on the individual; some people may find meaning in a career, while others may not. The point I'm trying to make, with difficulty, is that my life's work may be enough to supplement and override the loss of my "shattered world." It's interesting to note that I find my greatest doubts, insecurities, and concerns while I'm in school. It may be because I'm forced to think more about myself, and it could possibly be because I'm not realizing my career. This may be difficult to understand because it's difficult to explain.

I first noticed differences in my attitudes when I changed from school to work. In school I get tied up with day-to-day things and I think in terms of tests, papers, and grades. I tend to lose perspective of my career plans. I realize that school is a preparation for my career but it is not my career. This creates a sort of void or restlessness. It's like planning to paint your car. You're anxious to paint it, but you must put this off until you prepare the body.

Many college students have difficulty holding a belief in God. This is, I believe, why many have difficulty finding a meaning in their lives. In the past I've asked many of my college friends what religious affiliations they held. Some were agnostic, some atheist, some skeptical, and unconcerned, and some just not sure. It's easy to understand why they have those doubts because I've felt the same doubts. However, this is not the place to go philosophical or theological. I hold God as a value and hope I will continue to do so. The point here is that many people cannot find meaning in God. This often leads to free love with the accent completely on sex, rebellion in forms of delinquency and nonconformity, to a state of no achievement. I'm not against rebellion and nonconformity and, to a small degree, free love when it's goal-oriented, but to rebel and not conform as a reaction to giving up is wasteful. I want to stress here that in no way am I saying that everyone should find meaning in the value of God, but I am saying that everyone should find meaning! Everyone has a different meaning, although many people do find meaning through God.

I don't suffer in school, although at times I pretend I do, yet I do sacrifice. This sacrifice has a purpose—a meaning important only to myself—and when I have this purpose clearly in mind the sacrifice "ceases to be a sacrifice in some way." It takes on meaning! It should and can be this way in life. We are bound to suffer and to be unhappy; but if our attitude toward suffering is healthy, we will find a meaning in suffering.

In concluding, I would like to say that if I thought that all my suffering in school, at work, at home, or wherever I may be, had no goal, had no purpose, had no meaning; if I thought that I was nothing but a chemical reaction, a blob of protoplasm, a bunch of molecules, a modified *id*; if I thought I was born only to suffer and die, then I would *give up*. Although I can give no simple, logical meaning nor draw any new conclusion nor give any scientific or logical ways of defining my concept of meaning, I feel that one exists. It may be different to me than to you or others. It may change from time to time. I might never realize the meaning and only feel there is one.

FOUR REASONS

"Troubles of an early maturing male"

I believe that I live a unique life as, I assume, everyone does. But I believe I can substantiate my claims with the forceful statement that I have experienced all that there is to experience in life except marriage and my own death. Seriously, I believe in this statement; I may be limited in a lot of areas, but nevertheless I have the minimum basic experiences to validate my statement.

First, let me jump immediately to my early adolescent period around the age of 11 or 12 and pick out one instance in my life.

As I remember it, at this early date I never indulged in masturbation. My first wanderings and experiments in any sexual behavior took what I'd call an abnormal course. I will now state this abnormal sexual experience and then try to explain (to the best of my ability) why I ever behaved this way.

That particular first recognition and experience in sexual activity took place shortly after I had undergone all physical changes accompanying puberty and the transition to adolescence. This first experience consisted of my trying to force my bowel movement not to come out by pushing it back with my hand. And in connection with this I also used to insert into my anal opening articles that were in all cases (thank God) slender and long in shape.

To say these (more than once) early experiments were disturbing is an understatement. Even today I wonder what pleasure I got out of this, or whether I was completely nuts, or whether there is an answer to why I indulged in such behavior. Therefore, I believe it is necessary to look at some of the possible causes which resulted in that behavior. Some possible reasons are listed below:

1. I may have been definitely abnormal.
2. It may have some reference to my toilet training days.

    3. It may have been the result of inadequate knowledge of proper sex outlets and an ignorance in sex education as a whole.

    4. Or it may have been the result of a combination of factors involving sex-role identity, parent-child relations, religion, and anxiety feelings.

The first reason I definitely throw out. And mainly because I only indulged in this type of behavior for a period of two months. Also, after this brief period of two months, I returned to normal activity (which for me could only consist of sports), and put all sexual activity aside for the time being. I assume this sexually inactive period was normal (after my first experiences, it is a wonder I *ever* tried again).

The second reason or cause (toilet training) may have some bearing on the case, but I have no way of finding out how I was toilet trained. And if there is some connection between my behavior and toilet training, I can't see it at all too clearly. I was a bedwetter until I was 10 years old, but this seems to stem from other sources than toilet training (most likely my avid anxiety and aggression problems). One interesting idea I have formulated is that having come to adolescence, my already vivid rebellious attitudes were augmented greatly. And perhaps I reverted to my toilet training days where perhaps I had resisted authority not only by refusing to toilet train properly but more than likely by messing my pants as well. If that had been the case, then it seems to me that this idea in itself cannot be true. Because in my life now I am not exquisitely neat nor am I the opposite—a complete slob. This whole toilet training idea puzzles me greatly, and I can't figure it out.

The third reason is a little more sensible. My parents had never given me any insight in regard to sexual matters, nor even the basic facts. They had not prepared me for the sudden and demanding feelings I experienced in my early adolescence. I have since also discovered that none of my brothers and sisters ever received any sex education either.

I obtained most of my sex education via my male friends, and often with not a little embarrassment. One particular instance is very clear in my mind. It occurred at a place where all of the "guys" were having a bull session around the campfire.

The main topic of conversation was masturbation. This occurred about a year and a half after the bowel movement episodes. I got into the conversation by asking quite timidly what this was. The guys told me with a dazed look. I was 13-1/2 at this time and I was well developed for my age. I was a so-called early maturer. I did extremely well in sports and I was always fighting and winning. I was a ringleader for my age group, and they were shocked that I would be the one to ask such a question. In reply to their comment on what it was, I immediately replied, "Oh, so that's what it is!" and I continued by saying, "Sure." But in actuality, I had never had an orgasm and was next to ignorant on the whole subject.

What a blow my ego took. Here I was the toughest kid in my group and half the punks I had clobbered could masturbate and I couldn't. This *was* an embarrassing moment in my "sex education by buddies," but more so, it shows how really inadequate my whole knowledge of sex was. What made it seem even worse was the fact that I didn't start masturbating until I was 14 years old. A funny sidelight is the fact that after that discussion I would think of the dirtiest, most perverted daydreams, but I'd be darned if anything would happen.

It was a few months after that I had my first orgasm. It was through nocturnal emission and was accompanied by the usual erotic dream. However, when this occurred, I had already heard the term "wet dream," and I was not particularly affected, except that I loved it. It was shortly after this first orgasm that I started masturbating. Remember, for quite a while I had been trying my best to think up the most erotic daydreams in an effort to produce that white sticky stuff. Well, on this particular occasion I had been reading *Peyton Place* when all of a sudden it dawned on me that instead of imposing my will on my penis, I should impose my hand. Needless to say, I had some catching up to do and I proceeded with great vigor. From this point on, I only had relatively minor difficulties with heterosexual relationships, mainly guilt when I first indulged.

More than being a humorous narrative, the instances I have described show to what a large degree I had needed the proper sex education. I might also add a peculiar fact concerning this period and that was that I never once directed any questions on sex matters to either of my parents. What bearing does this seemingly insignificant fact have on the case we are studying? And this brings me to the fourth item on my list of reasons— the combination of factors.

In connection with the combination of factors, I would like to start with sex-role identification and proceed from there. But before I do another thing, I had better reveal some more of my private life and childhood.

Both my father and mother were strict my father more so. I would say that they were more than normally strict.

My father worked during the day, and being as strict as my parents were, we were all in bed by seven o'clock sharp each evening. Consequently, there was not much time to be spent with my father. I had an older brother who couldn't be bothered with his little brother. When I was born it was at a time when my nearest siblings were all girls, and if I was not playing with them at any time, I was more than likely being babied by one of them. And of course my mother was always present for me.

So we see early in my life where I may have had some problems identifying with the correct sex model. And although most arrows point in the direction that I would develop a very feminine sex role—I didn't! I believe that I don't have many, if any, feminine characteristics. I matured physically very early in adolescence. I was very aggressive, to the point that I was recommended for psychiatric care for getting into so many fights. I excelled in all areas considered masculine; I even developed fairly well-rounded heterosexual relationships. Then how did I turn out so "masculine" if my childhood was so dominated by "femininity..? My answer is that in being exposed to such an overdose of feminine sex-role models and feminine characteristics, I rebelled against them all. I asserted my masculinity even more forcefully and determinedly than I would have under normal conditions.

I believe that, untrained as I am, I really can't make a correct hypothesis, although this matter is one which I would thoroughly enjoy understanding.

I would say that parent-child relations, anxiety feelings, and excessive aggressive attitudes are all very closely related to each other and to the subject at hand.

My father died when I was 15 years old, and the relation of my aggressive behavior and anxiety feelings to this happening seems enormous, because it was shortly after my father died that I had the most trouble controlling them both. However, when I think back and take a better look at my childhood, I can see where the most pertinent reasons for overaggressiveness and anxiety had their origins much earlier than my father's death. When my father was alive I had a fair parent-child relationship with him, though it left much to be desired.

As I have previously mentioned, my father was always working. He had to spread his fatherly love out quite thin. Whenever he could, my father tried his best to spend as much time with me as he could. But more often than not, my father was mainly the authoritative hand of punishment. I did fear my father, of that there is no doubt. And it seemed that I never could please him. It was later on that I found out that, to the contrary, my father was always quite proud of me. He was so overwhelmed with worries and providing us with a roof over our heads that he simply could not express or show openly any feelings of pride that he felt for me. But regardless, the negation of feelings caused me to be alienated from my father and to fear him. Since I grew up with the feelings that I was never pleasing my father, I was even more motivated to do well in everything I tried.

Fear of my father may have caused me to keep my curiosity concerning sex well contained within myself and directed away from him. Well, if I could not talk to my father and if I had a wonderful mother-child relationship, then why didn't I approach my mother? Well, I obviously didn't and for two different reasons. The first concerns independence and the second concerns religion.

Having many children, neither of my parents could afford to baby us or be overprotective with any of us. In my case, even though my parents were strict, I was *very* independent. I would usually go off by myself each day (if I could ever get rid of my sisters) and be seen only at mealtimes, and, for the most part, I got a good smack for being late. This independence of mine was really quite strong. Even with this good relationship with my mother, I could never bring myself to become dependent on and confide in her. Even the time when I caught my penis in my zipper I had to half bleed to death before I'd tell either of my parents what happened.

In studying further this situation where I was always dependent on no one but myself and wouldn't even confide in my mother, I can see a correlation in the fact that there may have been and actually was a lack of nurturance in my infant and childhood days. When I examine my life then and now, I must admit I don't trust a blessed soul nor ever did. I might add in connection with this that I have always hated the world.

I'd give special consideration to this idea of a lack of nurturance and also to a previously expressed idea, the one of alienation from my father. It is these two concepts that I believe are the main bases for my excessive aggressiveness and often acute anxiety. It would be interesting to explore these two in depth, but suffice it to say, I haven't changed much at all and am still very aggressive, bitter, and anxious, to say the least. Besides, I want to return to the problem at hand—what were the possible causes for that peculiar behavior of my very early adolescence.

All of the issues that I am expounding—alienation, lack of nurturance, religion, and relative independence—are pertinent to the "case" in that they all acted in unison to keep me from confiding in or seeking answers from either my mother or my father in regard to the many questions I wanted to ask about sex.

I mentioned religion in connection with this discussion because I do feel that it plays a part. I am Catholic, and, in the Catholic religion, the confirmation ceremony occurs when the child is in the seventh or eighth grade and usually coincides roughly with the onset of puberty and the new feelings of sexuality accompanying it. Before you do get confirmed, there is an extensive preparation period which is supposed to rejuvenate any lag in your religious potential. Confirmation itself means that you have become a "soldier in the army of God." Despite my aggressiveness, my earlier adolescent and preadolescent days were fairly religious ones. And, with confirmation coming when it did, this bolstered all of my religious feeling. And during or just prior to this massive dose of religion, the behavior we have been discussing took place. I am not saying that religiousness is the cause of this behavior, but I do think that this brief period of high religiousness, at that particular time, was one of the contributing factors to why I never confided in or consulted anyone on sex.

My deep feelings on religion also made me feel quite guilty over this behavior and later on in my first explorations of heterosexual experiences. I mentioned earlier how I had loved my first orgasm (via nocturnal emission). Well, in that case I did, and not too many guilt feelings accompanied this at all. I had heard of wet dreams and I had also heard that they weren't considered a sin, but rather as nature taking its own course. Later, though, when I started masturbating, the feelings of guilt were something to cope with. And, to this day, I'd love to thrash the pious person who said sex isn't healthy and is a sin except when you are married. The troubled hours I used to spend mooning over imminent damnation were almost unbearable.

TO SHED A SHELL

"Struggling with inferiority feelings"

There are physical growth factors during middle childhood. By the time the average male is 12, he is 60 inches tall and weighs between 95 and 100 pounds. When I was 12, I was about 56 inches tall and weighed about 65 pounds. I guess I could be called a "late maturer." Usually a late-maturing male doesn't do well socially or athletically, so he puts all his spare time on 'his studies to advance academically, but in my case it wasn't so. As a matter of fact, I got average to poor marks throughout junior and senior high school. I wouldn't say that I wouldn't have done well athletically, but I didn't get a chance to prove myself because of my size. I didn't even make the Little League baseball teams because of physical and social reasons. I was too small and I was much too shy. I probably was so shy because of my size, and I let too many people dominate me. Some of the boys who tried out were not as good as I was, but they made the teams.

Influence of the family affects the individual in his middle childhood years. In my case, I was the youngest. Besides my mother and father, I had three older brothers and an older sister, who is also the oldest in the family. Between each child there is about four years, and I grew up in a neighborhood where there were no other children of my age and my brother closest to me in age was too old to play with because he was always that much more mature. I was always ordered around by my older brothers and sister, but I had no one younger than myself to order around. I believe I was about six years old before another boy of my age moved into the neighborhood. By this time, it was time to go to school anyway. In school I had a hard time getting adjusted, mainly because I was too shy. I would daydream a lot and the teacher would yell at me. I soon became terrified of teachers. I went to an old, small school. It was so small that we had two grades in each room. The teacher would alternate hours of instruction with each.

I think that when I went to school a great change came over me, mainly because I got to know certain peer groups. I became acquainted with children my own age, including girls, who terrified me, partly because they were all bigger than I.

As I passed into the adolescent period, I had some of the old problems and found some new ones. I was still the smartest boy in school. My friends were starting to excel in sports such as football and basketball. I was too light for football and too short for basketball. I needed something to prove my masculinity. Somewhere along the line, I found out that I could run fast. As a matter of fact, I was one of the fastest runners in high school. This solved one problem, but there were still others. The other boys were interested in girls now and were even dating. My parents reminded me constantly to stay away from girls until I finished school. I became very bashful when it came to talking to a girl. Stay away from them I did. I didn't have one date throughout high school. In fact, I was about the only boy who didn't go to the senior prom.

As I entered my sophomore year in high school, I was the same person I had been two or three years before. The only thing I had going for me was the fact that I was a good runner and an asset to the track team. But then I got pneumonia and had to give up all forms of recreation for a year. This sickness brought me down to 73 pounds. My doctor suggested that I lift weights to build myself up. Within two years I had put on about 50 pounds and added about eight inches in height. When my physical development advanced, so did my social development. You might say that I "came out of my shell" somewhat. I began to develop a personality and didn't find much trouble talking.

My parents may be the "old-fashioned" type, but there are some advantages that I received. For example, I don't smoke and am one of the few persons my age that doesn't. Also, I have stayed out of trouble, which is not the case with a lot of the "early-maturing" males. This is because they received more fredom when they were younger.

I am now 19 years of age, but I still have a few problems. Actually, I'm afraid to be 19 because I'm not mentally or socially equipped to be that age. Maybe I am. In fact, my biggest problem is the fact that I have a very bad inferiority complex, which has prevented me from being myself many times. My father has always gotten me jobs for the summer when I needed them. Whenever I went for an interview for a job or at school, he went along with me. I was never given a chance to be independent of my overprotective parents. Just in the past year or two have I begun to be somewhat independent.

I do not go out on too many dates, although I know and get along with a great many girls. Something that worries me is the fact that I have three brothers married and they went steady with their girlfriends for about five years. This puts me about two years behind schedule according to them.

Possibly my problems stem from the fact that I never developed a strong "ego identity" or self-concept in my adolescence. A number of psychologists and psychiatrists have pointed out that the adolescent in our culture is vitally concerned with assessing his liabilities and assets, trying on various roles to see which fit him the most comfortably. An adolescent, during this period, chooses long-term goals which will influence the course of his behavior for the rest of his life. Only a couple of years ago I finally decided what I wanted to be. Maybe I chose to be an educator because I want to give boys the chances I never had. Although I consider myself very skillful now in sports and acquire these skills very easily, these skills came to me late in my adolescence.

I have my certain goals in life all planned and am no longer afraid to go after them. Besides raising my own family, I would like to be a very successful teacher. The most important thing to me is that every boy gets a chance to prove himself, not only the ones with natural talent, but also the ones who have much room for improvement. There is nothing I hate more than a lazy student. I would like to be in a good education program in the school where I may work and catch problems while the kids are still young enough to do something about it; to develop them in mind, body, and spirit, and to make gentlemen of them.

CLOSE THE WINDOWS

" 'Caught up' in unrealistic attitudes"

I cannot conceive how a society so involved in the ideals of freedom of action and choice, so dedicated to the actions of making life more comfortable for the underprivileged peoples of the world, can adopt for its own members a cultural foundation so incongruous and conflicting. I have often wondered why citizens would allow them to remain functional for as long as they have. Perhaps there is some correlation between the two trains of thought. To me, this correlation is of little importance as compared to the desire to reconstruct our values. Little, in my opinion, has actually been done. But this is not the crux of my discussion, so I shall let it lie dormant for a while. After all, if we've let it go for so many years, a few minutes should not make a big difference.

As I recollect, the first time I was made aware of the strictness of our culture was when, at the age of 11, my mother and I had a detailed discussion of the facts of life. My sister, who was also included in the conversation, was about 10 years old. Although I had inquired as to where babies came from earlier (about age seven), the response then was not as enlightening.

The thing that remains the most poignant in my mind is not so much the information discussed (which I feel is seldom retained) as the manner in which we were informed. We had been told earlier in the day that my mother wanted us to come in from playing at 3:00 P.M. When we went into the living room, my mother told us to close the windows. This seemed strange seeing as how the weather was so warm. Yet she insisted. I know now that she didn't deem it wise to have the kids outside overhear the extent of the conversation. However, after hearing what she had to say, I felt that there was something secretive or even wrong with sex. At this point, it might be surmised by the reader that my mother's actions were but an individual example, not actually applicable as a manifestation of how our culture plays down the role of sex in our lives. I doubt this is the case. My mother is a woman whose ideas about sex are, in my opinion, very liberal. I feel that it is for the very reason that society pressures us to act in certain ways, contrary oftentimes to the manner in which we wish to act, that my mother was "forced" to act the way she did.

It has been stated by many psychologists that our culture is a conflict-arousing one. This can be seen in the culture's shifting of requirements for social acceptability in regard to relations with opposite sex peers. I remember that when I was about ten or eleven years old I had very little to do with girls. I was busy playing war or construction or any game which by its nature prevented girls from taking part. My friends and I used to spend some time ridiculing them or playing tricks on them. Some of them were quite clever. In one, for instance, we used to have one of the boys run up to a group of girls playing with their "sissy" dolls and inform them that if they left everything where it was and hurried over to a certain place (where they couldn't see their doll carriages), they would be able to see a real live dead cat. After some coaxing, they would usually leave. At this time, the rest of us would surreptitiously either hide their dolls or mess them up. We had a ball. We usually got away with it when the girls told the parents. We'd get a little scolding every now and then; but that was all. Boys our age were supposed to act like that. We were just normal kids growing up.

Then it seemed like everything changed. All of a sudden, a couple of the guys started paying quite a bit of attention to these girls; too much attention, as far as we were concerned. It was a while before the rest of us came around to the same line of thinking. During that time, we never quite got away with playing the same old tricks or making fun of the girls. All of a sudden, the parents were on the girls' side. They wanted us to treat them nicely, like little ladies.

During this time, there were a lot of conflicting ideas about our relations with girls. We'd even have to dress up and go to their birthday parties, treat them politely, and so forth. Our pride was shattered. We were degraded. Until we all changed our ideas about girls, we were under quite a bit of pressure.

Our interest in girls was brought about by the physiology of our bodies. Yet I can't help but think that it was also brought about, in part, by outside pressure.

Most of the conflict was brought about by our cultural dogmas. Was it or is it necessary? Is there a better way to go through this period?

When I was about 14 or so, I cannot be too precise about it, I went to parties with girls, enjoyed their company, liked to be thought of highly and admired for my masculinity by them. There was little actual tension or conflict that I am aware of in regard to the relationships, except the anxiety or nervousness in doing the right thing at the right time in their presence. As far as the sexual aspect is concerned, there was a progressive quality to the extent of holding hands or later even a good-night kiss.

It wasn't until I was about 16 that the more advanced stages of sexual behavior came to light. At parties I remember having the girl sitting on my lap with nothing other than kissing as the main order of the day. It was in progression from this that the petting came into being. I'm not saying that prior to this time there had been no petting or bodily contact. At earlier times, it was for curiosity or exploration. During the latter time period, it was done more for purely sexual gratification than anything else.

During this time, there was much information tossed into my face concerning the malignancy and immorality of sex. To my surprise, it came not so much from my parents as it did from outside sources. In school, my class (9th grade) got a lecture on how we should conduct ourselves at the annual spring dance. We had to force back the laughter, let alone the smiles. According to the teacher, we were hardly allowed to hold hands when we danced. We received this type of information from other public school teachers, as well. Once, our minister and his wife held separate meetings with the girls and boys of our youth group, the minister speaking to the boys, and his wife to the girls. Both adults were sincere in telling us of the evils of petting and necking. Most of the boys thought the whole talk was childish, including myself. I would say that although the listening body was a mixed age group (14 to 19), a good majority had already experienced much of what was being tabooed. However, I recollect taking notice of a few boys who were prime targets for such a discussion.

I don't want it to appear that I'm in favor of letting sex run wild, but I do feel that such discussions and lectures that are handed down by adults, and merely reflect the cultural pressures, are oftentimes quite harmful in forming adverse lines of reasoning in the younger child's mind in regard to sex. A possible example of this may be that at the end of our lectures, when we were invited to the rectary for refreshments, there was a strict line of segregation voluntarily set up by some of the girls and boys. Later on in the evening, this segragation was broken. Was it just a passing phase or did it leave, at least in some, a serious detriment in sexual terms of reasoning?

From this stage of adolescence until marriage, there appear a number of conflicting ideas and questions concerning the sexual relationships between opposite sex peers. These problems manifest themselves to a higher degree in the individual whose relationship with the opposite sex is limited to one girl. It is at this time that the specific information of functional organs, reproduction, and the like, is replaced (though never forgotten) by more intense problems. Questions such as "What is love?" "Is masturbation harmful in curbing sexual gratification?" "Is it right or wrong to have intercourse before marriage?" "Is petting right or wrong?" It seems to me that it is important to know how to use sex and what its limits are rather than to know that women are capable of supplying eggs which are known as ova.

Our culture seems adverse to all the physiological pressures exerted on the adolescent. This I can safely state, due to my own personal relations with the girl I intend to marry, and due to the many discussions I have had with people in the same situation. That there is a very definite conflict in our culture may be seen in the formation of a corresponding set of rules and philosophy by some adolescents. An example of what I mean is the statement which, by the way, is almost unanimously accepted, that "I don't care who the people are. If they've been going steady for over a year, they've had intercourse." This statement applies to people in the later adolescent stage, and although it has been noted that upper middle class adolescents are less likely to experience intercourse before marriage than those of a lower class, I have found this statement to be representative of a great many upper class people. You must realize that these ideas are not the result of documented experiments. However, I don't feel that they should be disregarded for this reason.

I should like to devote the next few paragraphs to a discussion of adolescents going steady—if I may be allowed to use a cliche—and those in the later adolescent/early adult status. I realize that many people never leave adolescence, but I do not feel it neccssary to be that technical in word choice at this time.

It is generally felt, from the adolescent's point of view, that people who are going steady experience several added conflicts, usually more anxiety-arousing, than "single" individuals. The most intense of these problems is that of deciding whether or not premarital sexual relations are right or wrong, and what actions are to be taken in regard to either reconciliation. Usually, either one of the two produces anxiety-arousing situations. I think most people will agree that deciding whether or not to have premarital sexual relations is in itself a main conflicting area for the adolescent, let alone planning one's actions accordingly.

Let us suppose that certain decisions have been reached on this question. Now let us see how, if at all, the answer will produce anxiety and conflict, and compare them later.

If the male has decided that it is not immoral to have intercourse, he has probably gone against the admonition and hope of his parents, as well as the cultural mores. There is a great deal of anxiety and tension involved. Once he has acted accordingly, he might resign himself to the fact that there is a chance that the girl may become pregnant. By this time, he may or may not have experienced the intensely conflicting and anxiety-arousing experience of fearing that his girl *might* be pregnant. He now plans on seeing that he and his girl friend do not indulge again (until marriage, of course). There is anxiety in trying to give up the pleasure he has enjoyed and taking into consideration the feelings of the girl.

But what if the male has decided that premarital sexual relations are immoral? There still remains the anxiety of having to consider a line of action contrary to the laws set by his parents and society. There is also the conflict over how to inhibit his desires and those of the girl, if he has any feelings whatsoever. Will masturbation successfully curb desire? Is it harmful? These questions and their answers are sure to produce psychological disturbances.

In regard to the degree to which these choices vary as anxiety-arousing situations, I doubt that there can be an accurate comparison because of the great number of differences in each of us.

In this "undocumented" discussion, I hope it can be seen that the most impressive fact formulated is that much of the anxiety and psychological disturbances are a product of the strict and contrary laws, customs, doctrines, and mores of our culture. A great deal of this tension could be avoided were it not for the narrow-minded, puritanical cultural traits that have endured for so long a time. If it were possible for the individual in our culture to more freely express the *natural* desires and actions attributed to the human animal for thousands of years, I feel that a general change for the better would take place in our society. The problem of morality in accord with sexuality alone plays such an important role in our lives that to twist and contort it to fit our so-called cultural heritage is to twist and contort the development of the inhabitants of the society itself. "Sex" is not a four-letter word. It should not be treated as such.

I'M LEARNING
THOUGH

"When idealism becomes a problem"

My parents, both strict Catholics, instilled in me a great respect for the church and its teachings. I have lived in a relatively small town all my life.

My father, a life-long resident of the same community, is quite well known. He had to turn down going to college to support his fatherless family. He often expresses his regret for not going to college later on. People in town often call me by my father's name and then excuse themselves.

My mother is the perfect lady. She is very quiet, yet in some ways wears the "pants." This in no way means she is masculine; in fact, she is extremely feminine, but she does handle the money in the family. I should not complain, for if it were not for her, I would not be attending college. She is extremely thrifty and saves every possible cent.

My childhood was normal, yet I must admit that my awareness of sex did not increase at a normal rate. I did not know the genital differences of the sexes until I was about 12. This unawareness can be attributed to the fact that the circumstances for observing the female body never arose. I didn't masturbate until 15 and didn't know what many of the sexually connotative words meant until about 18. I think that since I was so involved in other activities with the same type of children as myself, I was not overly observant of what went on.

As I said earlier, I was very active as a child. I coasted on snowy cold days for hours and hours, went on bicycle hikes, and played the usual children's games. I was on the Little and Pony League Baseball teams and played football, baseball, and basketball in my junior high years.

My high school years were productive in a social rather than a scholastic sense. My teachers continually complained that I did not work to the best of my ability. While in high school I wrote for the school paper and attended seminars in journalism at colleges and universities as my school representative. I was on the various dance and prom activites, and in the senior play and class day committee. My friends in high school were the football players, cheer leaders, class officers, and other school leaders. The other students ridiculed us behind our backs, calling us the clique running the student body. Our moment of triumph came at graduation ceremonies where we reaped the best scholarships. My friends later went on to college like Smith, Mt. Holyoke, Amherst, Dartmouth, Notre Dame, the Citadel, and Oberlin. We were not a vicious clique, as some felt, just a group of friends who had been buddies for years and naturally continued our friendships throughout high school.

Now, as a third-year college student, I am lost. I get depressed not knowing what's coming next. Following is an examination of my own problems as I see them and what relationship they have with my childhood.

During the past year, my conflicts with my family have inceased. While a young adolescent, my main problem was making a name for myself rather than being just "Bill's son"; my problem now consists of seeking greater independence. I want to go out and have a good time, come home when I want to, and be able to decide whether I want to take an apartment in town with some friends of mine. My parents seem to be unwilling to allow me to do the aforementioned things. Their argument is that as long as I'm living under their roof and receiving financial aid from them, I'll continue to do what they say. Whereas some shrink from argument, I fight violently with them. I maintain I'm able to make decisions maturely enough, and they are trying to hold on to me. I use what I learn in school as a substantiation of my argument. Immediately, my father replies, "Just because you're in college, don't think you know more than your mother and me." I think my father resents the fact that he didn't get the college education he wanted, and takes it out on me.

Along with this revolt against my parents for more independence, I have become increasingly lethargic in my church beliefs. For 12 years I was forced to attend religious classes against my will. The church and its principles represent a stumbling block to my free thinking and independence. I want to be free of everything, but this is impossible, for my conscience bothers me for every little infraction I commit, because I have to go to confession. But I feel so hypocritical because I know I'm going to do it again and again, so in the eyes of the church I don't receive absolution. If you don't get absolution and you die, you go to hell . . . ugh. (If my parents saw this they'd kill me.)

Another problem I've had the past year is the people who ridicule me for my lack of realness in my sexual and personal relationships. People often make remarks about sex and when I don't pick up the meanings, they say I'm anything from stupid, innocent, naive, to too idealistic. As I mentioned before, I never associated with people who talked about sex or used obscene language (notice I differentiate between the two) and naturally I don't know many of these terms. I'm learning, though, although I'm not going out and purposely trying to increase my knowledge of obscenity so I can be a "big" man. I was never really ashamed of this lack of knowledge, and I can learn the proper sexual terms from my mature friends and good textbooks on the subject.

Another point where people think I'm too idealistic is in my conversation, I abhor people who sit down and talk about others. When somebody is "cutting" someone I usually tell them to change the subject and this embarrasses them. People in this situation always jump to their own defense by saying, "Let's be realistic, people talk about me and you so we're not doing anything unusual." I feel that I don't really care what others say about me and I keep three things in mind:

1. I consider myself extremely loyal to my friends—I wouldn't believe anything about them unless they themselves told me and if I had anything to say about them I'd say it directly to them.
2. If I don't know them well I can't say anything and wouldn't believe anything about them until I was able to judge them myself.
3. And if I know and dislike them, I couldn't be bothered with such trivial conversation.

The defense that everybody talks about others is so foolish, but you would be surprised how many "free thinking" (ha) college students use such a defense. Today's college students are such joiners. Examples of these are those students who like folk music because to them those students that appear most "college" like folk music, and those who join the freedom marches but who really don't care what happens to the Negro.

The most alarming of my problems is the complete reversal of the type of friendships I'm making at school. In high school I had seven or eight very close friends; now I have about 68 friends, but none of them as intimate as my high school chums. I don't know whether I did this unconsciously fearing to be labeled as a clique member, but the change is very noticeable. When I remarked to a few of my classmates that I don't really have many friends, they usually reply, "What do you mean?" and "You're probably one of the most popular people in the class." But when I think of it, sure, I know and am known by many people, but how many can I really consider the type of friends one can confide his problems in. It is very distressing to me to be able to count them on one finger. This remains my biggest problem: should I sacrifice close friendships for greater popularity? This is a question only I can answer for myself.

THE HORROR
SHOW

"Why was I always so jealous?"

This is going to be a story of my life. I have never told anyone else a story of my life, so I think it might be interesting for both of us. You have probably heard other life stories before, so maybe this will be old hat to you. I hope not, because I really want to get this off my chest.

I'm not looking for sympathy or anything like that, but sometimes I think that I am, or was, crazy for some of the things that I have done in my life. I don't know, maybe they were all normal, but I never saw anyone else do such nutty things.

First of all, I will say that my home life was always the greatest. I have had everything that I ever wanted, within reason of course. I am the youngest child, so this probably explains why I got almost everything I wanted.

As a youngster I did about the same thing as every other kid. I got in fights, I threatened to run away from home a couple of times that I can remember, the same as any other kid. I disliked girls like all my friends did, but I can remember having a little girl as a friend for quite a while. This girl lived above me in the same house, so instead of being enemies we were friends. We used to play house and all that other rot that kids play.

Well, enough of that stuff. Now I will tell you about my older life. When I get through this paper, I will probably get a big kick out of it, as I know you will.

When I was in the second grade, my parents and I moved from the city to the country. When we were going to move, my father asked me if I wanted to move. I was overjoyed. When he said the country, I thought he meant a place like Texas or something like that. The thing that was in the back of my mind all the time was that there was no school in a place like that, so I would love to live there. Well, come to find out, there was a school . This really had an effect on me, I never wanted to go to school again.

It took me a while to get used to the change, but I got by. I always did well in school and got all A's because everything came so easily to me. This probably ruined me for life, because after I got out of grammar school I didn't do as well. As a matter of fact, I don't think I ever got more than one A at a time after those years.

My junior high years were a lot of fun. I can remember laughing more times at the stupidest things. It was great. Everything was a great big bowl of cherries then, No time for girls or anything like that as I was too busy laughing.

I can remember one thing in the eighth grade that had a lot to do with my later life. I met this girl named Jean. She was a great kid and I always used to talk to her during math class. That is where my trouble begins. I guess I kind of liked her because she was the first girl I ever really could talk to like a friend. She must have liked me too, because she told one of my friends she did.

I was too shy or something to ask her out or anything like that, so we were just friends, although I would have liked to have her as my girl friend like some of the other guys had. Nothing ever happened, though, not yet.

When I got to the ninth grade I started playing hockey. This was also a turning point in my life. After this, my whole life was hockey. I never studied or anything like that during hockey season. I loved the game and that was all. I still love hockey, but I don't let it interfere with my life like it used to do. I find quite a difference between high school and college athletics. Not only in the game itself but in the interest of the students. The kids in college just come to a game to get drunk and find themselves some action for that night.

Well, that has nothing to do with the subject at hand, so I'll forget it for now. Anyway, as I was saying, in the ninth grade I started playing ball. The freshman team was not very good, but I was picked to move up to the varsity for the last game of the season. This was a big deal and quite an honor. We lost the game, but I played a little bit.

I am not trying to brag about myself or make up stories by telling you this. What I am getting at is that being a good athlete made me pretty popular with the girls. I guess I was pretty good looking, too. That's what I heard, anyway. All right, a couple of girls wanted to go out with me, and I would have liked to take them out. You know something? I could never ask a girl out. I don't know what it was, I just couldn't do it. If I was at a party or something like that, I could do O.K. with a girl, but I could never ask one to go out with me and me alone.

Well, you can imagine what the girls started to think about me. You know, stuck up, snob, etc. I could almost have given a damn about them or anyone else, for that matter. This is when I took up drinking as a hobby. It was an outlet and sometimes the only thing to do. All of my friends did it too; we used to have a ball. This was only my sophomore year in high school. Oh, I must tell you that I never drank or smoked during hockey season. This is something I am still very proud of. It might not seem like much to you, but that proves how dedicated I was to hockey.

Well, things went on and in my junior year I ran into that girl Jean again. This time things were a little different. I was a little older and I knew a little more about life; you know, I was a little grown up. I took her out a few times, but I never really got serious with her. I took her to the junior prom and we went to an all-night party after the prom. Wait till you hear this. I was with her all night and I never kissed her once. Now doesn't that crack you right up? She was really nice stuff, too. I don't know why, but I didn't.

I had been out with other girls that meant nothing to me and had a good time with them, but because this girl really meant a lot to me, I could not touch her. I guess I was just shy or something. What a beaut I am anyway.

Now comes the real horror show of my high school years, my senior year. You wouldn't believe how much one guy could screw up. It was fantastic. But I will say one thing, I never had so much fun in all my life as that year. I would do the same things over again, with a few exceptions.

Well, in the end of my junior year I had rolled my car over several times (at once), so I lost my driver's license for an indefinite period. I didn't have a job and I just hung around the house or went to the beach all day. Well, do you know, this girl Jean came down my house and picked me up almost every day? She worked and paid for everything. What a great kid. I still treated her like dirt for some unknown reason.

Her birthday was in April so I decided to get a job and buy a present. I worked for a couple of days and made thirty dollars. This was on a Friday and her birthday was on a Tuesday. You guessed it. Every last cent gone in two days, all spent on beer and eats. Really a good time, but why did I do it? That's why I think I was a nut. Something was wrong. Normal people would not do a thing like that. She still stayed with me, though; she was a real sucker—either that or she liked me an awful lot.

In the fall we went back to school and soon it was hockey time again. I was the captain of the team and wanted the team to be the best one yet. We lost almost every game. No one but me and a couple of other kids gave a damn about winning. They just played for the glory and for the girls sitting in the stands.

Now I had a real grudge against the world and everyone in it. Jean was still around and still taking abuse from me. About this time she started to get a little sick of it. I don't blame her now, but then I wanted to kill her. I am very jealous and proud, I guess. Every time I saw her even talking to another guy I would start a big fight. We had more arguments, over such stupid things. I got real mad, too; I even hit her a couple of times.

Once she went out with a kid from out of town. I knew she was going to pull this so I followed them around and beat the devil out of the kid after he brought her home. This started a big fight between my school and the other kid's school. Real great. I almost landed in jail.

I could go on for hours and hours telling you the stupid things I did. Throwing bottles at her house, laying rubber in front of her house, swearing at her real bad; I don't know why I did all these crazy things, but I did.

Well, that about completes the story. Now I can't figure out why it all happened. Why was I always so jealous, so thick-headed, so possessive, etc.? I can't really find any reasons.

DOINGS

"Aggression, and a gang's mischief"

In this paper I plan to explain some of the actions of an adolescent gang or group (whichever you wish to call them). This group ranges from 17 to 19 years of age. These adolescents (including myself) have been around each other for seven years. Although now I am not around them as much as I used to be (about two or three years ago I would have considered myself an active member), I still hang around with them every once in a while. Because of the length of my association with this gang, I believe that I know it fairly well.

First of all, let me tell you a little about each of its primary members. The first member, Buff, is probably the leader because most of the kids usually find out what he is going to do before they plan to do anything. The reason for his popularity is because of his relatively pleasant, fun-loving attitude; besides, most of the good times have usually involved him.

Tim is slightly taller than most of the gang (about six feet, two inches); although he is well-liked, he has an explosive temper.

Mike's father died in the war. He already has a scholarship set aside for him if he wishes to go to college. He has been told that he has a very high I.Q. During grade school (grades one through nine) he received mostly A's and B's without any work; however, in high school he has frequently quit school entirely.

Bill is a five-foot, six-inch punkish-looking kid. By punkish I mean he even looks like a typical juvenile delinquent. You know what I mean, the long sideburns, etc.

I believe the factor that brought these kids together was the need for activity (excitement). At one time or another, there were more kids in this gang, but I noticed that whenever a kid finished his association with the gang (by this I mean he was still on friendly terms, but he was no longer an active factor in the gang), he no longer went in for the mischief that characterized the gang.

Through the early adolescent years, the gang's mischief consisted mostly of being in places and taking things that did not belong to us. For instance, playing in new houses under construction, using a cemetery as a playground, even though the police were frequently summoned to expel us, and hanging around old deserted buildings. Some of the things we took were materials for huts, or projects as cement tubs (industry used these to mix cement or chemicals in) which we used for boats. We might light fires in a field to clear it for a baseball field. Now this can be a sign of mischief, but then again most of these boys came from parents who had to work hard for their achievements.

Bill comes from the poorest family of the group, and the only time he ever got something he could use was when it benefited the family. Buff only received an allowance when his father sold a car (his father was an automobile dealer); also we always kidded him about how his father would always spend more money on the old car rather than buy a new one, and these cars used to really fall apart.

Although not everyone was willing to go along with the reason why we did something, everyone would go along just for the excitement. In looking for an explanation, I would say that we were just satisfying our want for things that might have been denied us. I believe we got our satisfaction from the fact that we were preventing someone from keeping something away from us. In short, you might say we were going against the limitations that our elders had imposed on us.

Now let me discuss aggression. During our youthful years (early adolescence) we were always active (a quest for excitement). We got rid of most of our aggression during this time through our participation in sports, for just about every one of us was active in sports (the school teams). When we were not playing among ourselves, we were always challenging other groups. (We usually always won.) As the years passed, our activities changed from outlets in sports to betting (cards, pool, etc.). Once again, however, this was characterized by fervent participation.

Once we reached high school, a change took place; since our physical activity had been more subdued, we indulged in more violent acts that just didn't make sense. Some examples were: breaking into a country club to steal four hundred dollars worth of booze; stealing one thousand dollars worth of golf equipment from another country club; often waiting for a truck carrying beer to stop for a delivery, then stealing the cases from the back of the truck; looting parking meters. Although we were not really tough guys, quite often one of the gang would deliberately pick a fight with someone who was much bigger than he.

I believe that this aggression is a replacement for the activity in the early years and a replacement for the participation in sports. Now as for the explanation for the need for activity, the reasons are probably many. We identified with a role that was too active. Thus in a sense you might say our fantasies became too much of a reality.

Buff, who in his earlier years was one of the kids who did it just for the excitement, has become more intensely identified with the gang. He is an intense gambler and is always ready to participate in a gang fight. At this moment his record reads: drunkenness, disturbing the peace, grand larceny. At this moment he is standing trial for breaking and entering and larceny. This is a good example of his gang identification in that we went along with two other kids' idea to rob a college dormitory.

Tim is now in the army. He was kicked out of the high school basketball team for arguing with the coach (maybe the coach represents parental discipline). He is the one who usually started most of the fights.

Mike has quit school and is standing trial for stealing a car and trying to run a police blockade. Although in the early years he was mild in his participation with the gang, since quitting school he has now developed the "buddy" attitude. By this I mean if my buddies are in a fight, it's my duty to help them; if my buddy is going to do this, I will too, etc. I think the gang is serving the purpose of his dead father; thus his male role is identification with the gang.

Bill now is engaged to be married and you would no longer consider him an active member. He is different from the rest of the members in that he comes from a large family. He is the second oldest; the oldest was a sister who got married before she finished high school. Even in his early adolescence he was the "show-off," the "wise guy"; he is always the one who will do something foolish. Although he never participates in gang fights, when he is picked on he always has to have a weapon. He was the first one to have a car and he makes good use of it. Another characteristic of his is that he is probably the heaviest drinker in the crowd. He is an attention-getter because of his unimportance in the family (since the youngest always gets the most attention). His excessive drinking, his need for a weapon when in a fight, and his use of a car are the ways that he proves that he is a man. Another thing to remember is, as I have already mentioned, he is relatively small in size and therefore is probably self-conscious.

ESCAPE INTO LONELINESS

"Fantasy is easier than life"

I can remember when I was young enough to want to sleep with my parents. I always felt uneasy when I was sleeping with both parents, but when my father left I felt more at ease. I can remember wanting to get closer to my mother only when my father left. At times she would move and I could feel how soft and warm she was, and I wanted to get closer to her, but I cannot remember ever doing this. Maybe this is why I am not as close to her now to talk to as I wish.

I do not remember too much of my earlier life except that I could always seem to get around my mother but not my father. I believe this had a definite effect on my later life and I will explain this later.

The deepest and most lasting impression made upon me by my parents was when I was in the sixth grade. My older brother was then in the tenth grade. A girl called him up on the phone and asked him to a dance. When my mother found out about this, there was a big argument in the house. My mother called the girl back and told her that it was not proper for a girl to call a boy. I cried all night because I was worrying about what the kids in school would say the next day.

From then on, until my graduation from high school, I was afraid to speak to girls. I knew that if they got to like me, then they might call and another argument might come.

When I was in the seventh grade, I met a girl that I liked. One day she came to my house. Now I really became scared: If my mother ever saw me with a girl, she would really get mad. Because of this fear, I chased the girl away and she never came back.

Another time, and with a different girl, the same thing happened. She told my friend that she liked me and was going to call me. Immediately I began to panic, so I told her that if *I* liked her, *I* would call her. I never called her and I was relieved when I came home and she didn't call.

As I am writing this, things seem to fit together for the first time. Now I can plainly see how early incidents can influence a person for years. I believe this to be one of the reasons I was so shy in school. That phone call made a deep and lasting impression on me. I also believe this incident to have had a remarkable effect on me when I was in high school.

I know that another reason for my being so shy was the fact that I had acne. I would think of this all the time and I envied anyone with clear skin. If anyone talked in front of me about acne, I would get nervous and scared. I was so self-conscious that when talking to a person I always kept my head down. I was brought to a point where I felt inferior to other people.

In high school I was also very awkward. I had identified myself with people in athletics. I read stories about Lou Gehring, Mickey Mantle, Yogi Berra, and Rocky Graziano. All these athletes were good at sports but very awkward and shy when it came to girls. If these men could gain social acceptance without having girls like them, then why couldn't I? I was a fairly good athlete, so I decided to try to become better and also pattern my life after these men. Since I was 11 years old I would pray every night to become a professional ballplayer.

At that time, I heard a minister talk about baseball players. He said the difference between the man who started and the one on the bench was the fact that one asked God's help. When I got to high school, basketball was my favorite sport. I would count the days until the first day of practice. I brought rubber balls to school and sometimes during class I would squeeze them to get stronger wrists. When I got home, I would take a ball and work with it till I was sore. At night I would dream of making great plays. Everything I did was directed toward my ultimate goal of becoming a professional player. I knew that if I was to become one I would have to at least make the varsity my freshman year. I didn't make it and I was worried and became disappointed; I would worry all the time. Maybe I was worrying because I wanted to prove to myself that there was a God. I knew that if someone like me could become a professional player, then only someone with great powers could bring this about.

When I became a junior I knew I could make the varsity, but I was still worried. I made the team but did poorly. But I thought at least here was a bit of a start.

My senior year I expected big things of myself. Each night I prayed to do well in games, but each day I did badly. At night I would cry because I knew that I would never make all-scholastic. All my prayers seemed to be wasted. I felt as though God had let me down.

I feel that the reason was because of my inferiority feelings and complete dependence on my parents. When I played baseball I would feel it was the pitcher against the batter. One man against one other. It was I who usually lost this battle. I also wrestled in high school, but I never won a match. One could say I was just a bad wrestler, but this was not the real reason. I know that when I stepped onto the mat, I felt inferior to my opponent and anxious. Here again, in a situation with one opponent versus just one other, I lost every match. When I played football, it was the same story. Here is a sport where 11 men work together. I had plenty of confidence in football, especially when I was carrying the ball, because the other men were there blocking for me. I was dependent on the other men; but there was always one thing I feared going into games. I was always afraid of having a man coming down the field and having just me between him and a touchdown. Again, here is a situation where one man is against just one other and it was this that I was always afraid of. In this situation, no one could help me. In hitting, no one could help me; and in wrestling, no one could help me. Here are three situations where I was all alone and it was this that I feared.

The wanting to become a professional athlete definitely affected my life. I wanted to make all-scholastic so much, but I failed and when I knew I would never make it, I almost went out of my mind with worry. This is why I do not have any real goals in sports any more. I may play them, but I never set a high goal for myself. If I did and failed, I would go through the same agony over again. Maybe this will keep me from becoming a better athlete and maybe people will call me a coward, but I know worrying does not do any good. I will just do the best I can and if I do well, then fine; but if I don't, the world will still go on spinning.

Because of my acne and my parents' restrictive attitude toward girls, I was in sort of a bind. During the weekends most of my friends were out on dates, but I was alone. I was afraid to meet girls because of my skin and my parents. At times, I would just sit in the dark and think. I wanted to be with people so much, but I was all alone. Then I would start thinking of a girl that was pretty. Even if she didn't like me, I pretended that she did and that she was my girlfriend. Like a child, I was living in a dream world. Physically I was 16 years old but acting childish. I remember holding my stomach and feeling nauseous. I felt empty and alone. Perhaps the only thing that would keep me from being lonely was a girl, but I was afraid of girls, and if I did have a girlfriend my parents would be mad. So I had an imaginary girl. For a year or more I had God's mother as my imaginary girl. This sounds stupid and confusing, so I will explain.

In the Catholic religion, God's mother is also called Mary or the Blessed Lady. I would always read stories about Her. One saint to whom She appeared said that She looked so beautiful and about 16 or 17 years old. I was always taught that She was very kind and understanding. What more could I ask for in a girl? If She is all I was taught, She wouldn't care how I looked.

I remember that my father was always very strict about things, but if I wanted anything I could get around my mother. Many times my mother would talk to my father and I would get what I wanted. This could be the reason why, whenever I prayed, I would always ask Mary's help. I would always go to Her first. Now that I am writing, I am also thinking. I know that I always wanted to be close to the Blessed Lady. Maybe in reality what I was doing was saying, "I want so much to be close to my mother, but I'm not really." I was taught also that Mary was our real mother and God was our real father. Because I was not as close to my mother as I wished, I made the Blessed Lady my real mother and tried to get as close to Her as I could

At times, I could talk to my mother about things that were close to me, but never to my father. Maybe this is why when I prayed, I very rarely asked God's help directly. I would always pray to the Blessed Lady to ask God for me.

Now that I had an imaginary girl, I felt a little better. I had a girl that my parents would never know about and one that didn't care how I looked. It helped for a while, but I still got lonely. There were times when I remember praying to see Her because I wanted something real, something alive. Most of all, I wanted someone to talk to and someone to talk to me. But this never happened. I never did see Her. I thought of Her a lot and what She must look like, but I never saw Her. I figured the next best thing to do was to paint a picture of what I thought She looked like. I spent hours trying to paint the kindest and most understanding face I could. These were the qualities that I wanted in a girl and this is what I needed most. If I went to my parents I would have gotten some, but not as much as I wanted. I would not go to them anyway, because I felt they wouldn't understand and I also had too much pride. Maybe this pride stems back to my early childhood when I wanted so much to be close to my mother in bed, but I would not give in. I would not go to her.

When I was not painting, I was writing about Mary. I tried to put my loneliness to some practical use. I wanted other people who were lonely to see what I had painted. Maybe they, too, could feel a little less lonely. I wanted to express my innermost thoughts and desires in a picture, in words, or in any way I could. I also wanted to show people how kind and beautiful the Mother of God really is. It was not beauty like the girls in Hollywood have. It was beauty of heart and soul that would far exceed any woman in the world.

This has affected my life in many ways. I am always praying to Her and sometimes I still feel that I could never really love a girl because I will be thinking of the Blessed Lady as my girl. The first girl I told I loved was a girl who was in a convent for three years. She came out and we started to date. Maybe I was looking for something in her that I saw in my imaginary girlfriend.

I do know where I want to go in life and why. I want to work with children. My parents very rarely sat down and talked to me. My father hardly ever spoke to me unless it was about gardening, which is his work. He is very quiet. Sometimes my mother talks to me, and when she does I love her so much. Usually she just yells and lectures like most mothers. If only they could try to understand me and listen to what I have to say without lecturing. If I could only once leave the house without their saying a hundred times, "Watch out driving," or "Don't be in late," I could love them so much more. I'd feel so much better if once they would just say, "Have a good time."

I always wanted my parents to talk to me about what I thought of most of the time and what I wanted to be in life. I remember once talking to my mother about something that was very close to me. She listened for a while and I loved her so much, but then she said I was crazy to think like I did. That really hurt me because it meant so much to me to have her understand. I wanted to tell somebody about my problems and how I thought, so I went to a priest. Priests were always kind. One priest in particular I remember best. He understood every thing I said. He was so kind and understanding that I decided I wanted to return this kindness and understanding to children who need it. This is the reason I want to work with children. If God wants, this is one goal I will achieve.

I have always wanted to express my innermost and deepest feelings whether it be painting, writing, or just plain talking. With children I will be able to express my deepest and innermost feeling—love.

If I am with children, I know I will have a tough time, but there will be moments when they will want me to listen to their innermost thoughts and dreams in life. It will be in these brief but very precious moments that I will have returned the kindness and understanding that was given me.

It will be here that I will not be alone any more. As long as I have people around, I am happy.

THE NEW MEMBER

"Sibling rivalry"

I don't think I can interpret my own behavior, but being able to look at incidents which have impressed me allows me to study it with some understanding. Truthfully, I don't feel that I have the amount of knowledge to be sure of my interpretations of any behavior, but perhaps this feeling is, to some extent, a defense to insure that I don't learn too much about myself.

My own family consists of my mother, father, and one younger brother. I really don't know what makes my parents "tick" because, so to speak, I am too close to the forest to see the trees. My father seems to be characterized by relative submission to and resentment of authority and a tendency to be prejudiced. This seems to fit with the impression I have that *his* father was very authoritarian. My mother seems much more independent in her actions and in some ways seems to rebel against authority. Some of this independence is evident in my behavior.

I was three years of age when my brother was born, and I can agree that the birth of a second child may have a detrimental effect upon the first. Looking back, I recall an incident which occurred when I was about four years old. When I heard my mother calling my brother's name, I rushed in from another room and clung to her skirt. She immediately told me to stop being "jealous." Now, I am sure I had no idea of the meaning of the word "jealous," but I can remember experiencing an immediate and intense feeling of guilt, so I must have known what she was referring to. This incident stands out above all others that I can readily recall during my preschool years and, although I might be wrong, I think the birth of my brother has greatly affected my personality. Before my mother had verbalized my exact feelings that day, I was vaguely aware of something that made me feel as though I had to compete with the new member of the family for attention and affection. Although I was allowed to hold the baby and help to dress and feed him, I still felt left out of something—he was the object of attention, not me—I only helped to give *him* attention. This blow to my emerging self-concept, this intruder called "the baby" was what I had been a few years earlier. How could I have ever been like him, I wondered, and besides, I was quick to notice, he possessed something which I didn't. Maybe I felt that he was more or less the object of attention because of this something which I lacked.

At any rate, my guilt feelings seem to have manifested themselves in a feeling of inferiority which I can recall vividly during my early school years, and less vividly, though I was still aware of it, as I grew older. I can remember being very critical of my looks, and when I was six years old the idea came to me that as soon as I was old enough I would pluck my eyebrows like my mother did so that I wouldn't be so awful to look at. On the first day of school, I was startled by the fact that three walls of the classroom were covered with blackboards, which, when I faced them, gave me the feeling that the walls were going to close in and crush me. Even now I have a tendency to fear small closed-in places and this might be an outgrowth of my guilt over feelings of jealousy—the idea that I am going to be punished for feeling this way.

I excelled in school work and was often in command of a group. My striving for excellence might have been an attempt to rid myself of feelings of inferiority. During these years I developed a need to cultivate a primary relationship with a peer. I was usually successful at this, and when our ways parted, I would establish a similar relationship with someone else, never feeling really complete when this person was not around. Attempts to prove myself not inferior are related to the fact that I could out-run, out-climb, and out-fight any boy in the neighborhood, not to speak of the girls.

With the onset of adolescence I experienced the usual difficulties, a new self-image and the desire for increased independence. My high school years were not abnormally difficult, however, and I surrounded myself with a group of girl friends and I always had one very close friend. What stands out during these years is the attitude with which I began to regard my studies. The desire for excellence was still there, but I decided that I couldn't be bothered exerting the effort required to achieve the highest grades. I had the ability, I felt, but I was lazy. I was still able to compete, especially with males, but holding myself back was a way of punishing myself in order to alleviate the guilt stemming from jealousy of my brother. At 15 I decided I would like to make a career in economics. By devoting myself to establishing a career I would be able to compete in what I already saw as a man's world. As time went on, however, the idea of devoting my life to a career seemed more unrealistic.

At 16 I started to work in a department store. One of my closest friends worked there, but we seldom saw each other and so I was alone, especially at break time, with people I had never met before, some my age, but most a rowdy group of older women. It was at this time that I started smoking. That was a miserable experience as I often nearly choked, and many were the times I had to rest my head on the table pretending to have a headache because I didn't want anyone to see my smoke-filled eyes watering. And still I persisted, because although it required using half a book of matches to get the thing lit, I could experience a feeling of completeness in the midst of all these strangers. (I still don't really enjoy smoking, but the idea of breaking the "habit" is one I rarely think of.)

My feelings of inferiority seem much less intense now, perhaps because they are more hidden. Some of the feeling is hidden behind a defensive attitude of indifference. My academic mediocrity might be a way of letting myself "have my cake and eat it too." Supposedly performing below capacity in some subjects is a way of punishing myself, but I will still obtain a college education which will allow me to feel somewhat superior. Then with marriage, hopefully, will come the permanent sense of completeness.

Although my brother and I are not extremely close, our relationship is a fairly good one. Now almost 15, he is living proof of much that has been said to characterize adolescence. First and foremost, he is a man, and if one is doubtful, the three whiskers on his chin will bear testimony to the fact. When

I asked him what animal he would most like to be, he replied, with some embarrassment, "The most playful animal, like a lion cub." This might be a reflection of conflicting desires to remain dependent and become independent. His actions are of interest to me because I passed through a similar stage not so very long ago. I am no longer aware of jealous feelings toward him; either they no longer exist or they have been hidden.

That his arrival has had an effect on my personality I have little doubt, but there are other aspects of my behavior that I am unable or unwilling to admit to or examine. Now that I have written this brief paper, I feel somewhat like a traitor to myself, but the thought has occurred to me that my reasons for writing about myself given at the beginning of the paper are just rationalizations. Perhaps admitting my guilt to the outside is another way of delivering myself for punishment.

1 2 3 4 5 6 7 8 9—RJC—82 81 80 79 78 77 76 75